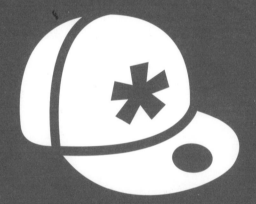

LITTLE MIX

ready to fly

Photography and Creative Direction
by Dean Freeman

Harper
Collins

INTRODUCTION

Hello and welcome to the first ever official Little Mix book! We've had so much fun writing about our younger years, style secrets, the tour, our *X Factor* days and each other, and we hope you'll enjoy reading it every bit as much as we've enjoyed putting it together.

Life with Little Mix has been non-stop since we won *The X Factor*. It's been amazing travelling around together and working on our debut album, and it feels so incredible to be getting our music out there whilst, hopefully, spreading a positive and uplifting message!

We just want to say thanks once again for all of your unbelievable support since day one. It may sound like a bit of a cliché, but without all of you we wouldn't be writing this right now. As a band we're happier and closer than ever and we've got such massive plans for the future. We'd love you to be there with us every step of the way.

Lots of love,

Jade, Leigh-Anne, Jesy and Perrie

1.
LIFE BEFORE
X FACTOR

LITTLE
YEARS

JADE: I was always quite a shy kid, until I got to know people. The only time I felt really confident was when I was performing. I started doing it when I was six, going to dance and theatre schools, and I loved it. I've got an older brother called Karl and we were really supportive of each other. I would always go and watch him playing football, and he would watch me perform. He's still really supportive and protective now. He always said I would be a singer and he believed in me from the start. In fact, all of my family have been amazingly supportive. I feel so, so lucky. My mam is my best friend – she used to take me everywhere, to every show. She must have spent a lot of money! I'm also really close to my dad. They've been there for me every step of the way.

When I was younger I used to sing at the old people's homes at Christmas and they used to go, 'Eee, pet, you're going to be a star one day!' I loved doing little shows like that because it made the people who lived there smile, and it was great experience.

I was a proper swot at school. My mam worked at my primary school so there I had to behave! I was quite an all-rounder. I loved maths and English and I always wanted to be the best I could be in whatever I did. I kept changing my mind about what I was going to do as a career. At first I wanted to be Diana Ross, then a forensic scientist, then a lawyer, then an English teacher and then an artist.

I was top of everything in secondary school but I still had no idea what I wanted to do long term. I loved dancing and singing, but I didn't see it as a realistic career, so I was always looking for a plan B.

I had loads of friends in primary school and I met lots of people through doing performing arts, but it was different when I got to secondary school. I was the only person from my primary school to move there, so I was totally on my own. It was awful. I went from being really popular to knowing absolutely no one. I really closed off from people and became super-sensible and quiet. I used to have my tie done right up to the top and all of my hair scraped back. I was like a normal spotty teenager. I worked really hard and went to all of my lessons, and people must have thought I was soft, because for the first two years at that school I got picked on quite badly. I was still going to tap and ballet classes until I was about 13, and I did drama at school, so that was my outlet when I was feeling upset or lonely. It gave me something to look forward to.

There was a time when I was bullied so badly by one girl that I bunked off school to avoid her, but in the end I told one of the teachers and thankfully it got sorted out.

I joined the choir and then in Year 9 my music teacher asked me to get up in assembly and sing, and despite being terrified I went for it. After that I gained more popularity and got more friends, and it was such a relief. My friends Holly, Anna and Sarah are still my best friends now. I know I can always rely on them totally. They really helped me be more confident with my singing and were so encouraging to me.

I started appearing in lots of musicals and plays, both in school and out of it, so that helped me to meet people too. I tried

---

PREVIOUS PAGE: *Jade practising her tap and ballet*

THE ONLY TIME I REALLY
FELT CONFIDENT WAS WHEN
I WAS PERFORMING

everything I could to get as much experience as possible when it came to performing, and it was a real release for me. By the end of secondary school I was head girl and everyone knew me because I'd been on *The X Factor*. I'd managed to take something really swotty and make it cool.

When I was 16 I started performing gigs in local pubs and clubs. I can't even count how many shows I did back then. I did everything that came my way. Around the same time I started going to house parties and being much more sociable, so I guess I had more of a balance. Singing always came first for me, though.

I first decided to try out for *The X Factor* in 2008. I was 15 and even though I did a lot of performing I was still a really nervous person. Singing was what gave me confidence, so I decided to give *The X Factor* a go. I didn't really know what I was doing; I literally just turned up and sang. I made it through to the first stage of Bootcamp, but then unfortunately I was sent home. I was heartbroken and I cried for weeks.

Simon told me to keep coming back as I was only young, but I took a break the next year to concentrate on my GCSEs.

I nearly didn't try out the next year either. I thought because Joe McElderry had won they wouldn't want someone from the same place again. But my mam encouraged me and I felt happier about

----

BELOW: Jade putting on an early performance
OPPOSITE: Jade on her fourth birthday

doing it because I kind of knew what I was doing. I got to the end of Bootcamp that time, but I didn't cry when I got cut because I'd already decided to come back the following year.

That same year I won the Pride of South Tyneside Young Performer of the Year 2010 Award, which felt like an amazing achievement and spurred me on to try for *The X Factor* one last time! At that time I was doing A-levels in English literature, fine art and media studies, and I was planning on doing a fine art degree, so that was going to be my back-up if I was cut from *The X Factor* again.

I was doing quite a lot of gigs around the North East. I mainly sang Motown tracks, because I grew up listening to that music thanks to my mam and my Great Auntie Norma. I was also teaching singing and dancing at a theatre school, so it was all good practice for the show.

JESY: I grew up around Essex with my younger brother Joe and my older brother and sister, Johnny and Jade. We lived in 12 different houses growing up, and even had a stint in Cornwall, but we moved back when my brothers got scouted for West Ham football club when I was 10.

We all really loved performing, and when I look back at videos from when we're younger we're all singing and dancing along to songs, and using whisks and hairbrushes as microphones. I

always thought Jade would end up being the performer, but she's now a football coach for West Ham and my brothers do building work with my uncle.

I was a funny little thing when I was small. I had really curly hair and I was quite eccentric. I looked a bit like Peter Andre's daughter Princess. I was always telling stories and putting on funny little accents. Looking back you could tell I was always going to be a performer. I was really confident and outgoing.

I guess I've always been quite theatrical and I started off wanting to be an actress, so aged eight I began going to a Saturday theatre school. Once I was in a performance of *Annie* and had to sing on my own, and my voice went all funny because I was so nervous. I think that really affected me and gave me a fear of singing. When you're dancing, nerves can be a good thing because they can give you extra energy, but when you're singing your throat dries up and you feel really panicked, and there's nothing worse.

When I was about 12 I went to the Sylvia Young Theatre School, which was in Marylebone then. Rita Ora was in my class, and Vanessa from The Saturdays was also there at the same time as me. That's when I first started beat boxing. I don't do it properly, I just kind of mess around, but I really enjoy it. There were three boys in school who used to do it all the time and I thought it was so cool, so I got them to teach me and I've done it ever since.

I loved Sylvia Young's, but a part of me didn't want to be branded as a stage-school kid because I always wanted to be myself. I didn't like being given elocution lessons and being told to speak properly.

We're all different, and the world would be boring if we were all the same. I didn't want to be something I wasn't.

After I left there I couldn't get into the schools I wanted to go to because they

----

OPPOSITE: Jesy and her brother Joe on holiday
BELOW: Jesy in a school photo aged five

were full, so I went to one near my house that I hated. I got picked on and I couldn't wait to leave. One of my teachers told me about this new school in Dagenham called Jo Richardson's which was just being built and was going to be special-ising in music and dance. I ended up going there for the last three years of my schooling, and that's when I got even more into music and drama.

At school the subjects I tried hardest in were the ones I loved, like drama, singing and dancing. I used to lose concentration in science and maths. To me there was no point in trying hard in those lessons, because I didn't want to be a mathema-tician or a scientist. My science teacher told me off for not working hard enough,

and I turned round and said that I didn't need science because I wanted to be a singer. He looked at me like I was mad, but I knew in my heart it was all I wanted.

Later on I got really into street dancing. The Diversity dance troupe who won *Britain's Got Talent* used to put on shows around the country, and one day I was in Lakeside Shopping Centre with my mum and they were performing. I told my mum I wanted to do what they did, but I never imagined I could. I went along to one of their classes and that was it. I was hooked. I joined the sister girl group called Out of the Shadows, and from then on it was all I wanted to do.

Before I auditioned for *The X Factor* I was working in a bar and really enjoying

it. I'd had quite a hard time from other girls at school, which gave my confidence a bit of a knock, but working in the bar and meeting so many people and having to interact with strangers really helped to build it up again. But I knew I couldn't do it for the rest of my life. I kept thinking about auditioning, but the only person I'd ever sung in front of was my best friend Solitaire, so I was really nervous about other people seeing me. I'd watched the show and seen the massive queues of people and thought I'd never have a chance. In the end she convinced me to go for it, and the next thing I knew I was filling out the form.

LEIGH-ANNE: It may seem hard to believe, but I was really shy as a child, and I always used to say to my dad, 'I don't like peoples!' I loved my mum and my dad, Debbie and John, and my older sisters, Sarah and Sian. But I was quite closed off from other people. I didn't have any hair for ages, so I used to look like a boy. Then, when it did grow, I got this huge afro that used to stick out all over the place!

My sister Sarah is an amazing performer, and we used to put on shows with my cousins. I remember we did a Spice Girls routine when I was about five. I was trying to copy everything Sarah was doing because I was so in awe of her.

The whole time I was growing up in High Wycombe I used to tell people that I was going to be a star. I think people thought I was crazy, but my family always believed in me. I took part in every play I could at school, like *Grease* and *Oliver!*. I also took part in a *Stars in Their Eyes* competition at primary school where I sang 'Ooh Stick You' by Daphne and Celeste.

I also went to the Sylvia Young Theatre School on a Saturday when I was 11, but it wasn't for me so I didn't stay long.

School was okay for me generally. I got teased a lot at primary school because I was never one of the 'cool' kids. I did hang around with a cool group, but I never really felt properly part of it. For some reason boys in particular were mean to me. But by the time I reached secondary school things changed a lot and I had a really solid group of friends who I'm still incredibly close to now. My best friend is called Hannah and she's the most supportive person ever. We're so close and we're always there for each other. I'm a bit of a party girl and we used to go raving together, to house parties or clubs. Hannah and I used to do spontaneous things like go to London for a night without knowing where we were going. I'm very much a live for the moment kind of person.

I loved music, drama, English and French at school. I was quite a good girl and rarely got into trouble. I did so many things growing up. While I was at secondary school I tried out acting, I played the drums for a while, learnt piano, had singing lessons – you name it, I gave it a go.

I took part in loads of talent shows, and I was also in a choir called Street Dreams and we used to busk in supermarkets to raise money for charity. I still support them now because they've done so much for me. I was also in a music company called Songbirds, which gave me some good experience.

PREVIOUS PAGE: Jesy aged ten
OPPOSITE: Leigh-Anne in a school photo aged four

After leaving school I got a job as an Aim Higher mentor for Year 8 students at my mum's school. I would help them to maintain their targets and concentrate on their studies and watch their progress. It was a really rewarding thing to do.

I stayed on for sixth form at my school to study for my A-levels in music, English and psychology, and while I was there I was made head girl. We had to have interviews for it and I must have done pretty well! My job was to be a good role model and set a good example for the younger students. That was good, because before I used to hate public speaking, and it really helped me to build up my confidence.

Just before I auditioned for *The X Factor* I was working as a waitress at Pizza Hut in High Wycombe, and I was planning to study educational studies at university if music didn't work out. I wanted to do a Postgraduate certificate in education and go into primary school teaching.

I used to save up all of my tips and travel to London to spend time in a recording studio called Atomic Studios with a producer named Jerome. I'd posted on Channel AKA a recording of '100 Days', a song that I'd made with an artist called Rampant. I started getting a bit of recognition off the back of that, and Jerome's brother rang me up and asked me if I wanted to go into the studio and work on some tracks.

Jerome used to make all of my beats for me, and we'd write together. I've been writing songs for years and years and I love it. I also worked with a guy named Varren Wade, who used to be in a band called Fun-Da-Mental, and with a girl named Katie Pearl who sang on the funky house track 'Something in the Air'.

I was really happy with the music I'd been working on as a solo artist, then one day Jerome said that I should be in a girl band. He probably meant it to be encouraging, but it made me cry, because I thought it meant that he didn't think I was good enough to make it on my own. I couldn't see myself as anything but a solo artist, but I didn't know what was around the corner …

OPPOSITE: Leigh-Anne as a baby
BELOW: Dreaming of being a star. Leigh-Anne singing karaoke at home on her eighth birthday

My dad had been telling me for years that I should audition for *The X Factor*, but my mum was putting me off because she was worried I'd be crushed if it didn't work out. Funnily enough, my dad then suggested that I get a girl band together, but I still wasn't into the idea. Some time later I was having one of those days when I didn't know what I was going to do with my life, so I sat down at my computer and filled out the *X Factor* application form. I just thought I had nothing to lose. Then I got a call to say I had an audition, which was a real shock. And that's when it all started.

✳ **PERRIE:** I was born in South Shields and I loved performing from a very young age. I get my love of singing from both of my parents because they both perform. My mum and dad broke up when I was young, so it was just me, my older brother Jonnie and my mum a lot of the time. But my mum and dad have always been super-supportive and we're really close. It's always been cool having two houses to hang out in as well. My brother Jonnie and I used to fight like cat and dog, but he was like a fatherly figure in my life and he really looked after me. We get on really well now.

We moved around quite a lot and even went to New Zealand for a while. We were

---

BELOW: Perrie aged two with her nan

there for just over a year when I was about 11, but we ended up moving back to the UK because sadly my granddad had a stroke so Mum wanted to be able to look after him. It's a lovely place, though, and I'd love to go back one day. I had some of the best times of my life there and I have so many amazing memories.

I had a really nice time growing up in the North East. I come across as quite 'out there', but in fact I was really shy as a child. I could talk when I was about eight months old, and my mum said that people used to find it dead weird that I could have conversations that young.

One of my earliest memories is from when I was a toddler. Mum was wheeling me through the Metro Centre in Gateshead in my pushchair and we saw some other young kids. They didn't have dummies so my mum said to me, 'Look Perrie, they don't need dummies because they're big girls. Are you a big girl?' I took my dummy out and threw it into a nearby pond because I'd seen people throwing money into it. Then I decided I wanted the dummy back and I screamed and screamed, so my poor mum had to take off her socks and shoes and go into the pond and get it back.

I first decided I wanted to be singer when I was about six. I was in the launderette with my mum and I stood up on one of the laundry machines and starting singing 'The Sun Will Come out Tomorrow' from *Annie*. All these old ladies who were in there washing their clothes were giving me 20p coins and I thought, 'Ooh, I'd like to do this for a living!'

I loved school, and when I was in primary I was real hard working and well behaved, but things started to slide a bit when I got to secondary school. I hated maths and science – unless they had the Bunsen burner going – and I was always trying to get out of PE. I used to stay with my dad every Wednesday, and I'd try and get him to write letters for me so I didn't have to do it, but my mum would always find out and make me go. I could always get away with lots more with my dad than I could with my mum. He's so much fun.

I wasn't at all sporty and I ran like a headless chicken. Sports Day was often on my birthday as well, and if so I wouldn't

LEFT: Perrie in her favourite red coat, aged two
OPPOSITE: Perrie on her mam's knee

go in to school because it totally ruined the day for me.

I loved English and I really enjoyed writing stories and poems, which I guess is a bit like writing songs. I joined the choir in my early teens but I never got the leads because I was too shy. Then later on I took drama for GCSE and I was Alice in *Alice in Wonderland*, which helped me with my confidence.

After school I went to Newcastle College to do Advanced Performing Arts and in the first year I had a real laugh. But in the second year I was in different classes to my friends and I felt really lonely. I was also always being told by my teachers that my voice was 'too pop', which was frustrating. But my form teacher, Steve, was so encouraging and he always made me feel like I was on the right path.

All I wanted to do as a career was sing, but I had to do dance in my classes as well so I got a bit knocked when I didn't do very well. But Steve helped me to get past that and keep focused on what I wanted.

While I was at college I decided to try out for *The X Factor*. I'd heard that they were doing auditions in Newcastle. My mum encouraged me to apply, so I went for it, thinking I had nothing to lose and everything to gain!

THE BIG
AUDITION

JADE: For some reason my audition in 2011 felt totally different to any of the ones I'd done before. I kept thinking in my head, 'It's third time lucky,' and I knew that if I didn't get through this time that was it, I wouldn't try again. It's horrible when you get knocked back and there's only so many times you can go in for something and keep getting turned away.

I was terrified about being told no in the very first round. If I fell at the first hurdle it would mean I was worse than I had been the previous couple of times I'd tried out.

Every other year I'd gone along trying to impress the judges and thought too much about what I was going to wear and sing, so I decided to totally be myself. I was wearing giraffe-patterned trousers and a little waistcoat and I probably looked a bit weird, but I didn't care!

Thankfully all of the judges said they liked me. Louis remembered me from before, and Tulisa said I must have had a lot of determination to keep coming back again. I sang an acoustic version of The Beatles' 'I Wanna Hold Your Hand', and Gary said he really liked it – and my voice and what I'd done with the track. I was so relieved. Kelly said she liked my voice but didn't think I was confident enough and that I should be in a girl group. I automatically pulled a face, then I remember Kelly saying, 'Hey, what's wrong with being in a girl band?' I thought she meant like a Kandy Rain-type band with sexy outfits – I would have hated doing that!

In the end I got four yes's and I should have been happy, but I kept thinking about what Kelly had said and wondered if she was right.

I was so happy I'd got through to Bootcamp again, but because that's where I'd been sent home before I felt wary and scared about going.

JESY: When I arrived for my first audition, which is one of the ones you do before you get to see the judges, there was literally a sea of people. I thought there was no way in hell I was getting through. I even asked my mum, Jan, if we could go home, but she was so encouraging. She believes that if you don't try, you don't get anywhere. She's always wanted me to be happy doing what I want to do.

I always like to be a bit different and a bit eccentric with what I wear, and I knew I had to stand out, so I wore some army combat shorts, stripy socks, Mickey Mouse trainers and a Donald Duck top.

I didn't want to sing something like Adele, because I knew everyone else would be doing that, so I chose a track called 'Bust Your Windows' by a lady called Jazmine Sullivan. I've got quite a soulful voice, so the song really suited me.

I was terrified doing that audition, because you have to go into a little booth with one person and sing to them. They're so close up to you and it's really embarrassing. You can hear all the other people auditioning around you too, which is so off-putting. I'd been told that they only give out a certain number of golden tickets – which guarantees your entry into the next round – so when three of the people ahead of me got golden tickets I calmed down a bit because I thought they'd probably given them all out anyway.

I walked in and told the guy in the booth my name and started singing. I could see him tapping his foot, then I beat boxed, and I think that's why I got through – because it was different from

what other girls had done. He handed me a golden ticket and I was in total shock. The guy told me to prepare some more songs for my main audition but to wear the same thing.

I had to be up at 6am to get to my main audition with the judges. My friends Shane and Solitaire and my mum were with me for support. I was third on stage out of everyone at the London dates, and I was terrified to the point where I was shaking and could hardly breathe. I couldn't bear the thought of the audience booing me or something. That would have been awful.

In the end it was all such a blur. I didn't see anyone in the audience, so it felt like it was just me and the judges in the room. After I sang I wanted to cry, because I knew it had gone wrong. Gary Barlow really didn't get me at all, and I remember being gutted. To me he seemed to be the Simon Cowell of the panel – the one that everyone wants to impress. He said he didn't like the audition and didn't think I had any potential whatsoever, and at that point I wanted the ground to swallow me up. I was mortified that everyone would see that bit when it was on telly.

Tulisa and Louis both said I had a lot of potential, and Kelly said she could see me in a girl group. Even that left me feeling really disheartened though because I thought it meant I wasn't good enough to do it on my own.

I came off with three yes's, but because Gary hadn't given me a thumbs up I still burst into tears. Dermot was hugging me backstage and asking if they were happy tears, but they weren't. I was absolutely gutted that he'd said no.

When I got home I became adamant that I wasn't going to go to Bootcamp because there was no point. My mum was desperately trying to convince me that I'd be okay, but I wasn't interested. In the end she told me I had nothing to lose, and I realised she was right. It would have been a massive opportunity missed.

LEIGH-ANNE: When the time came for me to go to my audition I was so nervous. I went along with a friend of mine called Jane, who was also trying out. We both got through the first round but then she didn't get any further and I was convinced I would go the same way. I couldn't believe it when I made it all the way to see the main judges.

When the time finally came to face Gary, Tulisa, Kelly and Louis I'd just got back from a holiday in Ibiza. I'd been partying quite a lot, so my voice was

suffering a bit. I was also really tired, and I felt cross with myself that I wasn't up to scratch.

I was wearing shorts, a vest top, socks and braces, and I was standing on stage looking out at the audience thinking, 'I'm never going to get through this.' I felt like I was watching the whole thing on TV. It was so weird. The first song I sang was Rihanna's 'Only Girl in the World', and then I sang the Gershwin song 'Summertime', which I'd heard sung by Ella Fitzgerald. I was so pleased that I got to sing two songs, because I think if I'd been judged on just one track I wouldn't have made it. Thankfully the feedback was really good. Gary said a star had been born, Louis said I had a lot of potential, Tulisa said I reminded her of a little Rihanna, and Kelly said she could see me in a girl band. That

was what Jerome had told me. I couldn't believe I was hearing it again!

I got four yes's and I was like, 'Come on, this is going to happen for me!' I knew if I got past that point I could go all the way.

✳ **PERRIE:** I remember being in bed at 4am one morning and my mum came and started nudging me to wake me up. I'm not a morning person so I wasn't happy! She told me that the Newcastle auditions had been cancelled so we'd have to travel to Glasgow there and then. I had to prepare a song to sing and find an outfit in next to no time.

I was so nervous that I nearly backed out, but my mum said, 'I've never asked you to do anything for me, but I want you to try and do this.' I really didn't want to

go, and I only agreed because I didn't want to let her down – and I said I wasn't going to tell anyone I was going.

I was wearing a little hippy dress and a headband and I felt like I must be sticking out like a sore thumb because everyone else was looking really cool, or wearing fancy-dress costumes to try and get noticed. I thought I looked too normal stood next to Superman!

In the end I got given a golden ticket after my first audition, which meant that I was through to the next round. That's when I thought there could be something in it after all!

Eventually I made it all the way through the initial three auditions, and then I had to wait to find out if I was going to sing in front of the judges. I was so happy, but so, so terrified.

When I got a call from *The X Factor* inviting me to audition for the judges I wanted to jump up and down and scream. I was shopping at the time with a friend of mine and I told her I'd got a call about a job interview. I still didn't want people to know I was auditioning, in case I didn't make it.

It was the best feeling being able to go home and tell my mum that I'd got through. She was so excited for me, and I was very happy – she'd promised to buy me an iPhone if I did well. It was a big incentive for me, because my phone was absolutely rubbish.

My family and I travelled all the way to Glasgow once again for the main audition, and everyone in the waiting room was singing dead loudly while they waited for their turn and seemed really confident.

I felt like I didn't deserve to be there. I was so timid and shy, and I was getting interviewed constantly. I was literally shaking, and I turned to my dad and said I didn't think I could go through with it. He turned round and said, 'Look, even I'd be nervous if I had to do those interviews. You're not used to doing them, but you know you can sing, so being on stage will be the easy part. Get up there and show them what you can do.' That totally stuck in my head.

Just as I was about to go out to perform I heard the *X Factor* theme music belting out and I thought I was going to be sick. Dermot was chatting to me and being really sweet, which made me feel calmer, but I was still feeling breathless.

When I was standing at the side of the stage waiting to go on, I saw the judges and it didn't feel like it was real. One of the researchers told us that the judges had given out loads of no's and wanted to see something special, so I walked out with a big smile on my face and waved to try and make an impression.

I sang 'You Oughta Know' by Alanis Morissette, and Tulisa stopped me pretty quickly. She and Louis didn't really like me, but Kelly said I'd blown the roof off the place, and Gary also liked me a lot. Tulisa said she wasn't blown away by me, and I was thinking that I was going to be sent home.

I sang Beyonce's 'Ave Maria' a cappella, and just before I hit a high note Kelly Rowland threw her pen in the air, and it hit Tulisa on the head! Everyone started arguing about me again and Kelly was whacking the table. Even though Louis and Tulisa weren't totally sure about me, I got four yes's in the end, and I ran off screaming and crying.

My family and I went and stayed in a hotel and had a nice dinner and it was so good. It was the best way to celebrate and one of the happiest moments of my life.

OPPOSITE: Jesy getting ready for The Brits

WE'RE ALL DIFFERENT AND THE WORLD WOULD BE BORING IF WE WERE ALL THE SAME

BONKERS BOOT-CAMP

JADE: Before going to Bootcamp I decided to go for some hypnotherapy to calm my nerves. I never used to get nervous when I sang in pubs and clubs, because it was all about having a good time and most people were drunk when you sang in front of them, but when you do *The X Factor* you're being judged and it means so much. I learnt different techniques to calm myself, and one of them involved tapping different parts of my body – I must have looked a right weirdo doing that before I went up on stage!

The first night of Bootcamp was crazy. Everyone had a big party in one of the hotels, and funnily enough some of the only people who left and went to bed early were me, Jesy, Perrie and Leigh-Anne.

We all knew that opportunities like that don't come along often, and I didn't want to blow it for the sake of a party.

The next day a huge chunk of the contestants got sent home, and when I looked at who it was, most of them were the ones who had been partying late. I think it was a bit of a test for everyone involved.

I was put in a few groups with a real mixture of people. I was hanging out a lot with Johnny Robinson, who is so lovely. I was moved from group to group and told no three times, and my head was all over the place. It was one of the best and worst experiences I've ever had.

BELOW: *X Factor* tour outfits

Several of us were told that we were good but we weren't strong or confident enough, and that's when they decided to try and put together some girl groups. At first I didn't like the idea at all, but as soon as I was put with Jesy and Leigh-Anne it felt right, because we were already sort of friends.

I was aware of Perrie as well, because she's from the same area as me and we know a lot of the same people. I'd tried to track her down but I hadn't been able to, then I ended up sitting next to her when they were divvying up the groups and we got on straight away. She was worried that her look was really different and she didn't fit in with anyone. At one point she was crying and I really felt for her. I remember wishing that she could have joined up with us.

Jesy then got moved into Perrie's group, and all of a sudden we were rivals. Leigh-Anne and I had never heard Perrie sing, and when we did ... wow! We thought we had no chance compared to Perrie and Jesy's group, but then neither of our groups got picked.

At that moment I just knew we were going to get put together. For some reason I had this gut feeling. It sounds cheesy but I do think it was fate.

JESY: I both loved and hated the whole Bootcamp experience. It gives you so much more passion when you see how passionate everyone else is about it. I grew in confidence so much too. I met loads of brilliant people, including Derry, who told me he'd auditioned so many times and got no's and still carried on. That showed me how silly I was to nearly give up so early on. I think in this industry

you've got to keep going even when people say no.

I got knocked back three times before we got put in the band, so it was disheartening at times, but I kept picking myself back up again. I was so determined to show Gary that I did have potential.

At first I was put in a group with loads of boys for the initial task, and when we performed before the judges Gary was smiling when it came to my part. He later said that he had seen a lot of people at auditions that he didn't think were good enough to go through, but he'd since changed his mind about them after seeing them at Bootcamp. I was like 'Yeah!' – I was well happy.

I was feeling hopeful after that, but then Louis called us back on stage and said none of us had star quality. My heart sank. The thought of going home and telling everyone I hadn't got through was so horrible. I went off stage and I was sobbing. All the cameras were in my face but I didn't want to talk to anyone. I went into the toilet and sat there and cried and cried. My sister Jade called me, and I had to tell her I'd been sent home. She offered to come and pick me up and I was so grateful – I just wanted to get out of there.

One of the researchers came in to see me and gave me a cuddle and asked me if I'd do an interview, but I didn't want to be on camera crying. She said she'd come back in ten minutes, and I was planning to do a runner so I would get away without doing it. Then she came back in and said it was best for me if I stayed. I was in two

----

OPPOSITE: Jesy and Leigh-Anne at the sound check for the tour

minds, but she said it was for my own good, so I was intrigued.

In the end I agreed and when I walked out I saw about 30 people standing around. We got told they were going to choose some people to put in a group, and I was praying they'd choose me. Originally the thought of being in a group would have horrified me, but now the idea of having to go through the whole audition process again the following year felt so much worse. I would have done anything to stay.

When my name got called out I was so happy. My poor sister was waiting outside for me. She was desperately trying to call me while I was waiting to hear my fate, but I didn't answer my phone. She must have felt as confused as I did.

I was put in a group with Jade and Leigh-Anne, and we sat up until four in the morning rehearsing that night, even though we had to get up at six. Then I got taken out of that group and put with three other girls, including Perrie, and I was gutted because one of the girls was very open about the fact that she didn't want to work with us. Jade, Leigh-Anne and I had worked so hard together and I thought we'd had a really good chance at making it through.

In the end both of our groups got rejected so I decided that was that. Then out of nowhere Jade, Leigh-Anne, Perrie and I got put together and I could not believe it. I kept thinking, 'How many chances am I going to get?' But as soon as we sang together it just worked.

I know Jade's already said it, but it was like fate. Leigh-Anne and I shared a room at Bootcamp, then we met Jade and became really good friends with her,

and then we met Perrie when I was put in the band with her. It was so strange how it worked out.

I would hate to be a solo singer again now. I don't know how people like Amelia and Mischa get on stage and sing on their own. I would be so scared. The girls are like my safety net, and I don't get nervous the way I used to, because I know we've all got each other's backs.

LEIGH-ANNE: I carried on waitressing after my audition, and I also applied to university so I would have something to fall back on if *The X Factor* didn't work out. But I couldn't wait to get to Bootcamp.

When I got there I was surrounded by all these amazing singers and I started to doubt myself, because I didn't see why I would get chosen out of all of those talented people. Then when I had to perform I don't know what happened, but something came out of me and I started jumping around on stage and really going for it. Something clicked and I knew I had to get through it. It felt like my one shot to do it. Then we got put into groups and we had to perform together, and I enjoyed that so much more than I thought I would. For the first time I began to wonder if there could be something about being in a girl band after all.

I was so gutted when I got a no after the first Bootcamp challenge. I got my belongings together and was ready to leave, but then a group of us got asked to stay, and I knew that I was going to get asked to be in a girl group.

I was put with Jade and Jesy, and then they took Jesy out and put a girl called Shanty in our group. She was lovely and we worked really well together, so I was

49

gutted she didn't go through. But I shared a room with Jesy at Bootcamp and we'd got on so well and been a great support for each other. Also Jade and Jesy had been told before that they'd be good in a girl band, so we'd planned to stick together so the judges could see how well we worked together.

Jesy got put in a group with Perrie and we knew it was either our group or theirs that would go through, because we were too alike for them to choose both. I was stunned when we were both given no's, but then they called Jesy, Perrie, Jade and me back on to the stage and said they wanted us to be a band. That's when I realised one hundred per cent that I had to be in a group – especially with the other three girls. I loved having other people to support me.

After being so introverted as a child, it's so weird to think that now I perform to thousands of people and I don't get nervous. My confidence is growing all the time, and I credit the girls with a lot of that because they've boosted me whenever I've got down or doubted myself.

I used to get so nervous when I was a solo artist, and I never felt I properly performed. I would just stand there feeling really nervous. It was like there was something missing. Now I feel as if I've found my place. I know where I belong and there's a special spark between us all. I was meant to be with these girls.

We were so happy when we found out that Tulisa was going to be looking after groups, because she's the judge we really wanted to work with. We felt she believed in us from the start and she was so down to earth and lovely. She was like the final piece of the Little Mix puzzle.

I FEEL AS I'VE FOUND MY PLACE

✳ **PERRIE:** I'd got through the auditions and I was beside myself with excitement, but now it was time to try and make it through to the next round. It was all about the preparation.

I learnt six songs for Bootcamp, and my mum took me shopping to get me some new clothes. She told me I had to look immaculate, and we got loads of amazing stuff. She even bought me some new headphones so I could listen to my songs on the way to London.

When we got back from shopping I laid all of my outfits out on the living-room floor, and I burst into tears because I knew I'd feel so guilty if I didn't get through. We didn't have much money and yet my mum had spent all of this money on me because she believed in me so much. That made me feel so emotional. She said to me, 'I just want you to do well. Even if you don't get through, I want my baby to look good on telly!'

Bootcamp was actually the worst experience of my life. I had no friends, because everyone I made friends with kept getting booted off. We were staying in various hotels and I felt really lonely because I had no one to hang out with.

As the other girls have explained, we all got three no's pretty much straight away, and I was so tired from trying so hard. It was like an emotional roller-coaster, and there were several times when I really wanted to walk away from it. But I knew that if I did, the cameras would follow me and it would all be shown on TV and I would be mortified.

I didn't know if I was coming or going half the time. I rang my mum and said that I'd never been so depressed in my life. I was really overtired and drained and I wasn't eating enough because I was sick with nerves.

I didn't eat for about three days straight, and then I made friends with a girl called Sarah and also Andy from The Risk. I felt so happy to finally have some friends that I instantly started to feel better and went and ate loads of food. I've never felt that stressed in my life. It takes a lot for me not to eat!

When Jade, Jesy, Leigh-Anne and I were all called back on to the stage I had no idea what to think. Initially Jesy and I were in tears because we didn't understand what was going on and we were so exhausted and confused. Then Kelly asked if we thought we could be in a group together and we were like 'Gosh, yes!' We were so happy.

I couldn't imagine how I would get on with people in a group, as I'd never done it before. I never thought I would meet girls as crazy as me. I'm a bit cuckoo, but they're all exactly the same, so it just worked.

OPPOSITE: Signing the tour programme at a meet and greet on the *X Factor* tour

BIG
BONDING

✳ **PERRIE:** We discussed everything and we decided that we needed to spend some serious time together and practise before Judges' Houses, as we didn't know each other very well. We knew we needed that really close bond if we were going to click as performers. We all went to my house in Newcastle, and from the word go it was like having three sisters. My mum cooked for us and we had girlie DVD nights and it was so much fun. That's one of the most fun weeks of my life. But that's not to say we didn't work hard. We barely paused for breath. Apart from Jade who kept taking Sudoku breaks. I think it calmed her down!

My family loved having the girls around, and when I look back on that week it holds such incredible memories. That was when it all really started and when Little Mix were officially created, so whatever happens in the future that will still be one of my favourite times I've ever had with the band.

🎀 **JADE:** We did just get on so well at Perrie's and it felt so easy. It wasn't like it was any effort. We liked the same kind of music and we've all got the same sense of humour. We told each other all of our secrets and talked about everything. It was definitely like having three new best friends and like we'd been a group forever. We all sat down together and we worked out what would set us apart from other girl groups. We asked each other who we loved and looked up to when we were growing up, and we went from there. The first thing that came into our heads were the Spice Girls. Girls and boys loved them and there was no jealousy towards them, and we wanted to be like that too. We're

four individuals and that was one of our main strengths.

We realised very quickly that we were on to something special. We could all sing, we could move, we all scrubbed up well, and I knew that *The X Factor* hadn't seen a group like us before.

🎧 **LEIGH-ANNE:** Hanging out at Perrie's was such a laugh. We stayed on the floor together and laughed and sang constantly. The first few days were spent getting to know each other, then we had a Skype chat with Tulisa, and from then on things got serious. We were up at seven every morning and if we had even a five-minute break we'd feel guilty and get straight back to it.

We came up with new arrangements for songs, and my favourite was when we mixed Michael Bublé and Justin Timberlake's versions of 'Cry Me a River' together. We were being so creative while working out whose voices did what. We knew we had to be different from other girl bands, so we tried everything, and Jesy's beat boxing brought something totally new and fresh to all the tracks we rehearsed.

We explored every avenue we could to improve on what we already had. We travelled around a lot and kept coming up with more and more ideas. We even went to Jesy's old school to work with her music teacher. It was such an intense period of time that by the end of it we knew each other inside out, which is exactly what we needed when we were faced with the next step – Judges' Houses.

📻 **JESY:** Perrie's house is where we properly bonded as a group. Me, Jade

and Leigh-Anne had already grown close because we'd been together before in the earlier band, so Perrie could have felt out of the loop, but it was all so natural. Perrie's so easy to get along with. It sounds really, really cheesy, but I love the girls to pieces and they're like my family, and it all felt so right from the word go. They're the most genuine, lovely people I know. I didn't have that many friends at school, I think because I was different, so I feel so lucky to have met the girls.

We all love TLC and En Vogue and Destiny's Child. We looked up to them because they were so talented and they worked so hard, and we decided that we wanted to try and capture some of their sound. I don't think I had ever worked as hard as I did that week, or had so much fun. Once we started harmonising and coming up with ideas there was no stopping us. We were feeling so positive about the future and we couldn't wait to showcase all the tracks we'd been working on.

BELOW: Backstage on the tour

AIN'T NO MAN
MOVE LIKE JAGGER
A NIGHT TO REMEMBER
SWEET CHILD OF MINE
SWEET DREAMS
JAR OF HEARTS
ROLLING IN THE DEEP
WHO YOU ARE
CAN'T GET YOU OUT OF MY HEAD
SINCE YOU'VE BEEN GONE
CHINA IN YOUR HAND
REET PETITE
HIGHER AND HIGHER

PROUD MARY
GIRLS JUST WANNA HAVE FUN
SHE SAID
FIX YOU
HEY YA
SEVEN NATIONS ARMY
SET FIRE TO THE RAIN
THAT OLE DEVIL CALLED LOVE
EDGE OF GLORY
THE SHOW MUST GO ON
YOU GOT THE LOVE
BEAUTIFUL
SUPERBASS
ET
DON'T LET GO
CANNONBALL
FINAL MASH - UP

JUDGES' HOUSES

JADE: After the excitement of the weeks leading up to Judges' Houses we crumbled a bit when we actually got there. We had so much confidence beforehand, but even though we knew we had something special, when we were faced with everyone else we panicked. How could we compete with the really good-looking boy bands? We thought we had no chance. Girls love boy bands, and there were some great ones.

PERRIE: It wasn't like we were just showing friends and family what we could do; this was in front of all of the *X Factor* crew and a massive audience.

JESY: I really like Greece. I'd been the year before for a holiday with my friend Dilem and we had such a good time. It was amazing being in Crete, but it also gave us a real taste of what life could be like if we did well, so it made us even more determined – and even more nervous.

PERRIE: I think some people thought Crete was going to be a bit of a jolly since we were getting to go somewhere hot and lovely, but there was very little time for fun. Every spare moment was spent rehearsing.

LEIGH-ANNE: We wanted to be the kind of group that you watched and thought, 'They are bringing something completely new and different. They're not like anyone else we've seen.'

JESY: We'd had a few ups and downs with changes to our chosen songs in the run-up, so we felt a bit all over the place because of that. Our name also got changed the day before Judges' Houses started. We had been called Infinite Bass, but the producers didn't think it was right for us, and we became Rhythmix, at least for the time being. So we did feel a bit unsettled.

LEIGH-ANNE: We'd had everything planned, so the changes came as a bit of a shock. But we bonded even more while we were there because things were so intense.

JESY: Obviously we knew that Tulisa was the groups' mentor, but we had no idea who her guest judge was going to be. We thought it might be Dappy or Tinie Tempah. There was a rumour in some magazines that it was going to be Jessie J, and when we walked out and saw her we all had huge smiles on our faces because we're massive fans, especially Leigh-Anne and me. Tulisa asked if we were excited and if we liked Greece, and we were all like 'Yeeeeees!' Jessie J joked that we would have preferred to go to Romford, which is my home town, and then high-fived me. Having a laugh like that put me at ease a bit, but as soon as we started to sing, things got properly serious.

LEIGH-ANNE: Obviously there was even more pressure because Jessie J was there – we all idolise her. Tulisa and Jessie both do the kind of music we love and our music has a similar style to theirs.

JADE: We performed Fergie's 'Big Girls Don't Cry', and by the end of it we were so terrified that our mouths went totally dry and Jesy lost her voice. Tulisa was sat there wearing shades, so it was impossible to read her face until right at the end.

JESY: I looked over and saw Tulisa and Jessie smiling, which was amazing. But then as soon as we finished Perrie and I were crying. I was worried that I'd messed up the end of the song and I was desperate not to let the other girls down.

LEIGH-ANNE: We also sang our mash-up of 'Cry Me a River'. The sun was in our eyes and we didn't have enough room to do the dance routine we'd put together, so we felt really deflated. In fact we cried our eyes out when we walked away afterwards, because we

thought we'd blown it. Everyone there was amazing, so now we were doubting ourselves. Because everyone else was so good it knocked our confidence a bit.

PERRIE: Tulisa said we had something different about us and an urban edge, which was really positive. But she also said that she worried about us being so young, and whether we'd be ready for the competition.

JADE: I had already thought that Tulisa would say we were too young and not ready, and then she said those exact words! I was so gutted.

BELOW: Jade eating her favourite dish, lasagne

THERE WAS NO STOPPING US

LEIGH-ANNE: I saw Jade's face drop when Tulisa said it. We were crying to Dermot because we thought we had blown it.

PERRIE: I cried so much while I was in Crete. We were all convinced that we weren't as good as the other groups. Some of them had been together for years, but we'd only had a few weeks to get ourselves ready. Everyone else seemed to be feeling really happy with their performances, and there was us being total wrecks.

JADE: We knew that if we didn't make it through it could potentially mean the end of the band. We didn't have enough money to go to each other's homes or travel up to London all the time. It just wasn't realistic. We had become so close that I couldn't imagine not being with the girls any more. The thought of it broke my heart.

LEIGH-ANNE: Waiting to hear our fate was awful. Also we got on really well with all of the other groups, so it was doubly hard because, even though it was a competition, we all wanted each other to do well.

JESY: We'd already been so disappointed during Bootcamp with everything that had gone on, and we wanted a yes so badly.

PERRIE: We barely slept that night because we were all crying and wondering how we were going to tell our families we hadn't made it. The next day we had to walk up this big mountain to face Tulisa again. I'm so lazy that I remember thinking, 'I'm a person, not a goat!' We were all shaking, but we knew we'd done all we could. There was no point in being dramatic; the decisions had been made.

JADE: I had said to the others that if Tulisa starts by saying something really nice there will be a 'but' afterwards and we won't have got through. So when she said, 'Girls, I think you did really well yesterday, but …', I was thinking, 'There is no way I'm going home. I have not come back here for three years to be sent home again.' I was gearing up to tell her she was wrong. I'd already got the speech rehearsed in my head. As we stood there in front of her we had no idea which way it would go. Then I heard Tulisa say, 'I'm really sorry …' and I put my head in my hands. Then she said, 'You're going to have to do this all over again!' – I was nearly sick!

LEIGH-ANNE: We all were jumping up and down and screaming, and then Tulisa came over and gave us a hug and it was the best feeling in the world.

JESY: When Tulisa said, 'We're going to have to see you in the live finals,' our mouths dropped open. We knew we had so much potential but we were convinced we hadn't got through.

PERRIE: I screamed and then we jumped into the pool. We nearly drowned – we didn't realise it was salt water and it was in our mouths and eyes. I don't think I looked my best!

LEIGH-ANNE: We didn't actually celebrate properly while we were out there. We were so tired after everything that we celebrated by sleeping that night!

JADE: We had to share a plane back with everyone else, so out of respect for the bands who didn't get through we didn't want to be jumping around and being loud. But none of us could stop smiling.

PERRIE: All I could think was 'Thanks, Mum, for making me go to the auditions in the first place!' The best bit for me was when we were all standing round and I called my mum and put her on loudspeaker and we all screamed, 'We're through!' down the phone. What a moment!

JESY: I think it took a while for it to totally sink in. It wasn't until a bit later that I thought, 'Oh my God, we're going to be in the *X Factor* live shows.' We could not *wait* to get started.

MOVING ON IN

JESY: When we got back from Greece we stayed in a hotel in central London overnight and then moved straight into the *X Factor* house in Hertfordshire the next day. I was really missing my mum because I'd barely seen her. I think we were all feeling a little bit homesick, and we knew we could potentially be in the house for some time.

LEIGH-ANNE: It was wicked moving into the *X Factor* house. We got on really well with all of the other acts, but we were so close from day one that we spent a lot of time together. We understood each other like sisters, and it was amazing to be going through everything with girls who totally got how you were feeling.

JESY: We got so used to being together in the end that if we got separated we didn't like it. I remember this one time when we had to go and stay in a hotel and we were all given separate rooms, and I was crying because I missed the girls!

JADE: We did bicker every now and again, which is normal. But it was about sisterly stuff like who's next in the shower and who's moved the straighteners. Really silly things that don't matter at all, and it would all be forgotten about in a matter of seconds. We want to make sure it stays that way. We've got to remember

----

BELOW: Jesy and Perrie messing around backstage

how lucky we are to have this opportunity, and we don't want to ruin it with arguing.

PERRIE: We soon found out who the messy ones were when we shared a room together – all of us! It's quite embarrassing really. At first we were sharing with all of the girls, so there were 13 of us in one room. You can imagine what that was like. It was crazy. But the beds and the pillows and everything were out of this world and we were so tired all the time that as soon as we got into bed I was gone. I love sleeping anyway and it was heaven.

JESY: I was so used to just being with the girls that it was strange having other people around – especially 13 girls with one bathroom and one mirror. It was good fun, but it was complete madness as well. There was stuff everywhere. As more and more people left the competition, other acts moved into their rooms, so in the end the four of us ended up on our own again. We were in this massive room on our own, and we had our own balcony and everything.

LEIGH-ANNE: Jesy was the tidiest out of all of us in the house probably, but that's changed now. We all used to feel a bit ashamed when we looked over at her corner and it was all nice and clean and organised.

JADE: I did try and keep my things tidy, but when there are four girls sharing a room it's never going to happen, is it? We were all borrowing each other's things and buying new things all the time, so it definitely wasn't the best-kept room in the house.

PERRIE: Because I wanted to sleep as much as possible, planning was called for when it came to getting up and out each morning. I'd try and lay clothes out the night before, which was supposed to help keep things organised. But then it would end up with us all getting up at the same time and literally throwing all our clothes around, trying to decide what to wear. It was chaos. Everyone tried to mother me, and they were always shouting at me to get me up in the morning. Sophie Habibis used to pull my duvet off, but nothing worked. We did have to grow up a lot, though. We were doing things like food shopping without the help of our mams, so I was buying all sorts of things. My bags were full of chocolate cakes, sweet waffles, Golden Syrup – you name it. We didn't eat terribly healthily in there. It was like we were unleashed, so I had to rein myself in a bit at times.

JADE: We all loved going shopping to the supermarket and stocking up. It was one of our favourite things to do. However, we had a funny moment in a supermarket just weeks before the live finals. Everyone else was already really well known and we wanted to see if anyone recognised us. As a bit of a test we went to the local Tesco and not one single person knew who we were. We got all giggly as we waited for someone to clock us. Maybe we should have done a little song and dance or something to see if that rang any bells?

LEIGH-ANNE: We were in the house for about three weeks before the show started and that time was pretty magical.

PERRIE: I swear, everyone thought they were on holiday in those first weeks, because we had a games room and big tellys and we were all cooking together and partying.

JESY: There was so much involved in the preparation. It's not like you just go into the house and then the live shows start. We spent about three or four weeks getting everything sorted out. I loved it when we filmed the opening credits for the show in this big studio in London. We were standing in front of a huge fan and we felt so glamorous. It was really dramatic. And it was amazing and hilarious to hear the voiceover man say our name for the first time.

JADE: As we neared the first live week the tension rose. The whole atmosphere changed and you could tell that people were feeling really nervous. Everyone stepped things up a gear and started rehearsing more seriously than they ever had before. We spent loads of time in the studio learning songs and dance routines, and as much as everyone enjoyed it, things got scarier as Week 1 rolled around.

PERRIE: People started to bicker a bit more. We used to get treats in the house, like going to a concert or a show, because we were working so hard. We were offered tickets for the musical *We Will Rock You*, but we decided not to go because we wanted to put in some more rehearsal time. Everyone thought we were mad! Anyway we offered the tickets to some of the other acts, and all of a sudden a big argument broke out about who was going to go. I think everyone was feeling a bit cooped up and wanted a break, which was why people sometimes got a bit stressed.

JESY: Things definitely began to change as time went on in terms of competitiveness. You could tell that people were starting to take it more seriously and see each other as proper competition. When you're in the house it's like being in another world, because you don't really see anything outside of the house and the studios. You don't even watch TV or have time to call your family, so it's easy to get a touch of cabin fever, which can send people a bit crazy!

MAKE-
OVER
MADNESS

JESY: As soon as we had our make-overs we felt even more like a band, and we loved the fact that they didn't want to totally change our style and make us something we're not. They liked the style we already had, so they gave us tweaks rather than any massive image overhaul, which we wouldn't have been happy about. We wanted to stay 'us'.

Leigh-Anne took one for the team with her new style, bless her. Funnily enough, when we were talking after Judges' Houses about what they might do to us when it came to the makeovers, Leigh-Anne wanted to go blonde and I wanted to go red, but they did it the other way round. Leigh-Anne had even been joking that they were going to shave her head, and then weirdly they did! I didn't have anything too dramatic done, but I didn't love having the ends of mine so blonde. I was pleased when I was able to do what I wanted with it again, and now I love experimenting. As for the clothes, I liked some outfits and hated others. Some fitted in with songs we were doing, so we went along with it even if we didn't love them, but looking back we did have a few shockers!

LEIGH-ANNE: When they first told me they were going to shave half of my hair off I was terrified. At first I really didn't want it done, but in the end I actually thought it looked quite cool. Although I do remember sitting there at one point holding half of my hair in my hand and feeling so gutted. I liked the style when I was on the show, because it was different and it was like my 'thing' to have the crazy red hair, but I regret it a bit now because

I'm trying to grow it out and it feels like it's taking forever.

Styling wise, at first we kind of wore that we were told to, but as the competition progressed we got more confident about what we did and didn't want to wear. We do work with stylists, but even now we still wear our own clothes a lot and we never wear things we're not comfortable with.

PERRIE: I really didn't want my hair cut off, but I knew that makeovers were a big part of the competition and I expected something dramatic to be done, so I went with it. I was having my hair done for eight hours the first day, and then I had to go back on the second day to get more done. I didn't know hair could even take that long!

Just before they snipped my hair I was stroking it and saying, 'We'll be together again soon.' I've always had good hair because my mum's a hairdresser and she's done it for me my whole life, so to say goodbye to it was so hard. I had extensions put in, but a month down the line they really hurt, so they were taken out. That's when it hit me how short my hair now was. It had broken off a lot because it had been dyed white blonde, and the extensions had also ripped some of it out. I was literally left with a pixie crop. I called my mum and she told me to sleep in some treatment to help get my hair back in better condition. I'll never get extensions done again, and I'll get my mum to do my hair for ever more! Leigh-Anne's was obviously the most extreme. When they said they were going to shave half of her hair off I really felt for her, but I knew she would be able to carry it off.

JADE: The makeovers were among the things that everyone was looking forward to when we all moved into the house, and we were no different. We worked with Jamie, the chief hairdresser, Natalya, the head make-up artist, and Laury, who was in charge of styling.

I really wanted a bit of a change, so when they suggested I dye my hair purple I was happy to go for it as that's my favourite colour. It reminded me of the makeover episode of *America's Next Top Model*. They always do some quite 'out there' things on that show, so I thought they would really go to town on us.

I loved getting my make-up done too. We learnt some really good tips. Natalya put some amazing colours on us, and after she'd done it once we wanted her to do more and more and to try crazier things.

It was funny when we got to the 'glamour' shoot, which is the picture you see at the beginning of the show each week. I used to practise posing in the mirror at home, imagining what it would be like to actually do it – and now here I was!

GOING LIIIIIIVE!

JESY: Ahead of Week 1 we did a big press conference at the ITV studios, where we met loads of journalists. People were treating us like we were celebrities, which was so odd because we didn't feel like that at all.

LEIGH-ANNE: It was our first proper taste of what it must be like to be famous and have paps taking your photo and stuff. It was mad.

PERRIE: We were sat in a room with loads of journalists and we were asked all kinds of questions. We got interviewed by *This Morning* and by Lorraine too. It gave us a really good idea of what's expected of us from the media.

JESY: We were so excited about our performance in Week 1 and we wanted to make it fun, which is why we decided to sing Nicki Minaj's 'Super Bass'. The theme was Britain versus America, and it's just such a storming song we knew it would make an impression.

LEIGH-ANNE: We'd come up with our own arrangement for the track, and I think people were really impressed with us because it was clear that we wanted to bring something new.

PERRIE: We wanted to get everyone up and dancing, having a good time and enjoying it as much as we were. The first performance was so important because it was what we were going to be properly judged on.

JADE: We would have been utterly gutted if we'd gone home that first week, so we worked incredibly hard to make everything perfect. Tulisa told us to stay calm and said that we didn't need to worry because we knew exactly what we were doing, but the nerves did still kick in backstage.

JESY: Before we went on stage that first week we got really worked up, and then realised that we were taking things too far. We decided we needed to chill out a bit, and so we started doing this silly face at each other where we pull our top lip up to show our teeth. It became our jokey trademark, and we still do it now whenever we're feeling a bit stressed, because it always makes us laugh.

LEIGH-ANNE: Jesy also used to do funny accents before we went on stage to calm us down, which seemed to get more extreme as the weeks went on. She used to do this hilarious *Braveheart* accent and we'd be in stitches. We helped each other out with our nerves.

PERRIE: We didn't want nerves to get the better of us, because that's when things go wrong, so we decided to treat it as fun and said that as long as we put everything into it, we couldn't go wrong.

JADE: Standing on stage waiting for our music to start was surreal. They played our VT, and looking out into the audience I could see all of our families – that's when it hit home that this was for real. We had the best time ever on stage and we were jumping around like lunatics. Louis said we'd come a long way from Bootcamp, and at that moment we really felt that too.

PERRIE: Louis also said we had brilliant chemistry and that although girl bands don't traditionally do well in *The X Factor*, we could be the ones to change that.

LEIGH-ANNE: Kelly gave us some constructive criticism, which we were happy to take, and Gary Barlow said that we were already the best girl band ever to appear on *The X Factor*. I literally had to pinch myself.

JADE: But despite getting great comments the pressure was on more than ever because of the big twist. When we found out that four of the acts were being sent home, we knew we had to give two hundred per cent if we wanted to stay.

LEIGH-ANNE: We were so scared when we heard about four acts being sent home. We didn't know if the fact that there was no public vote was a good thing or not, but we were happy with the feedback we got, so we just kept everything crossed. We almost felt like people expected us to go home because we were a girl band, so we had even more to prove. There had been a conversation in the house really early on where everyone was speculating about who would go home in the first week, and several people said it would be us because girl bands don't do well. That didn't make us feel great! No one seemed to have any faith in us staying past Week 1, and that made us doubt ourselves. Even good friends of ours told us we were amazing but that we had a big job on to make people like us and get girls on our side.

PERRIE: When Sunday night rolled around we knew it was make or break for us, and it felt like we were waiting an eternity to find out if we'd been chosen to stay or not. When it was announced that we were coming back the next week because Tulisa had saved us, we were … I can't even put into words how happy we were.

JESY: We were gutted that Two Shoes went. They were like big sisters to us and looked after us. They were such lovely people inside and out and so talented too. I couldn't believe it when they didn't get through.

JADE: By Week 2 we were feeling much more settled and finding our feet. We had a schedule every week where we would go to vocal rehearsals and choreography, so there was lots of getting up early, ready to face the day! We were getting on the coach at 6.30 in the morning sometimes. But then sometimes we'd head straight to styling and they would put on make-up for us and do our hair and make us look much better! But other times we were just doing it ourselves, so there would be sunglasses and a lot of concealer going on.

PERRIE: That second week it felt like we had hours instead of a week to prepare, because everything went so quickly. For our second performance we wanted to try and keep it funky and fresh and in our own style. We wanted every show to be like a Little Mix party – or a Rhythmix party, as that's who we still were at this point!

LEIGH-ANNE: It was the first public vote, so we had to step things up even more if we wanted to stay in, and we needed to choose a great song to fit in with the theme, which was Love and Heartbreak. We didn't want to do a ballad, so we needed something funky. Our fate was in the public's hands!

JESY: Everyone kept talking about the curse of the girl band again, which piled on the pressure. But we also thought, 'Why *can't* a girl band win?' In the end we knew we'd worked hard and we could only do our best. The song that we chose was Nelly Furtado's 'I'm Like a Bird', but we definitely funked it up and put our own slant on it. We had an amazing rhythm going on in the background.

JADE: We had so much fun during the performance and Tulisa gave us a standing ovation and told us we'd smashed it. Louis agreed with Gary and said that we were the best girl band ever to be on the show and that we could be the next big thing. Kelly said we should be proud of ourselves, and Gary called us fresh and exciting and said we were individual, which is exactly what we were aiming for.

JESY: All we could do on the Sunday night was hope for the best and pray that people were supporting us. It was only the second week, so of course we didn't want to go home. We never wanted to go

----

OPPOSITE: Sound check on the revolving stage

home! But it would have been a massive blow to go that early in the competition. When we were standing on stage waiting to hear the results from Dermot we were petrified. All I was aware of was that he was calling out names and ours wasn't there. So when he did call out 'Rhythmix!' we all collapsed.

LEIGH-ANNE: We were so sad to see Nu Vibe go. We'd got really close to them – I think because of the whole group thing. We all came together and shared the experience of being in Greece together and then making it to the live shows. Tulisa always said she wanted all the groups to be like a little family and support each other, which is what we did. To see them go was heartbreaking. I was in tears for ages.

PERRIE: We sensed right away how different the energy in the house was without them there. They were young, crazy, fun lads and they made the house more exciting, so you could tell instantly that they weren't around.

JESY: They could be annoying at times because they were so energetic and full on, but they were badly missed. They were genuinely lovely, lovely boys.

PERRIE: The longer we were in the competition, the closer and closer we all got. We were like a family. We used to spend loads of time in our room just chatting and hanging out whenever we

---

BELOW: Leigh-Anne and Ashford from The Risk, backstage on the *X Factor* tour

got a chance, and we'd get so excited we'd almost wet ourselves.

LEIGH-ANNE: We all bring out the best in each other. The competition was so tough this year, and when we were in front of the judges it was good to have the others there in case one of us had a meltdown!

JESY: The other girls are like my legs – I'd be lost without them!

JADE: Tulisa became a big part of our group early on and was the best mentor ever. When she used to come round to the house we'd just chill out like mates. To us she's our big sister and hopefully always will be.

LEIGH-ANNE: We were really excited about doing rock week.

PERRIE: I was actually named after Steve Perry from Journey because my parents were massive fans, so I feel like rock is a part of me.

JADE: And my mam had a motorbike – if that counts! I think people thought that rock would be a bit of a challenge for us because it's not our usual sound, but we embraced it and rocked it out on stage.

JESY: We sang Ke$ha's 'Tik Tok' and definitely turned it into something of our own. We mixed in 'Push It' by Salt 'n' Pepa, who are one of the best girl bands of all time. And in the end I think we did totally rock!

LEIGH-ANNE: Louis said the song wasn't rocky enough, but he did comment on how well we get on and said we could be really, really big. Kelly said our look needed pulling together, and then Gary and Tulisa had a bit of an argument about whether or not the song was properly rock. But as far as we're concerned we took a song and made it totally rock, and we loved every second of it.

JADE: I think the comments were pretty fair. We didn't want to do a classic rock song, though; we wanted to do something different.

JESY: We're young and I think it's cool that we took a young, fresh song and made it rocky. That's who we are.

LEIGH-ANNE: We were, as usual, so happy to still be in the competition when the results show came to a close on the Sunday, but we were so shocked that Kitty and Sami were in the bottom two, because they've both got such amazing voices and both of their performances were really good. But at the same time, everybody was amazing.

PERRIE: The bottom two result was always going to be a shock, because we loved everyone and we knew how hard everyone was working. We just kept crossing our fingers that we would keep coming back.

ALL CHANGE

JESY: In Week 4 we ended up changing our name from Rhythmix to Little Mix, and weirdly we got used to pretty quickly.

JADE: There was already a charity called Rhythmix, so we had to find an alternative. We knew whatever we chose we would have it for all of the time that we're together – which will hopefully be forever! – so we had to choose carefully. After going through loads of ideas we finally settled on Little Mix, and we're really happy with it.

LEIGH-ANNE: Our fans got used to it quickly too. We were getting such amazing support, especially from girls who were turning up to the studios to meet us. That was definitely a massive boost for us, especially during Week 4 when something really horrible happened.

JESY: I was seen breaking down on the show over some comments that had been written about me on the internet. I was really trying to be brave, but when someone picks up on your insecurities it's really tough – especially when they write things on websites for everyone to see. I did my best to ignore the things that were said, but it wore me down. When you're in a band with three beautiful girls who are obviously a lot slimmer and smaller, it's really hard when people make such a big deal of it. I just didn't know why people needed to be so mean. I didn't get it. I'm a normal size 10–12 girl and I know I'm not perfect, but who is? The big thing for me is that I didn't want it to give a negative message to young girls who watch the show and might read something where someone says I'm too big. I don't want anyone to ever feel that they're not good enough. It's just bullying at the end of the day – by people who aren't brave enough to say something to your face. I kind of knew before I went on to the show that I might get some nasty comments because I'm not stick thin, but it's so hurtful when you see it.

JADE: Jesy is one of the most beautiful and nicest people I've ever met and I can't understand why anyone would want to be mean to her. She's amazing, she's talented, and she's gorgeous. The thing about us is that as a band we're not trying to be sexy and perfect. That's not what we're about. One boy wrote on Twitter that the reason we come across as sexy sometimes is because we're not trying to be. I was bullied at school, so I know on some level how horrible it feels, although obviously what happened with Jesy was magnified by a million. It made me so, so angry, because I knew I couldn't do anything to stop it. If we were to hit back on Twitter we would have looked just as bad. I would die for Jesy's figure, and all of the people who slated her are mad.

LEIGH-ANNE: I think we are good role models, and people who watch us can see that, whether it's teenagers or mums of young kids.

PERRIE: I was fuming about the whole thing. Who has the right to pick on someone like that? How dare they?

PREVIOUS PAGE: Jesy's clothes and trainers, backstage on the *X Factor* tour
OPPOSITE: Jade at final rehearsals, with curlers in her hair

I was sitting and looking at her one day and thinking how gorgeous she is, and I couldn't understand what these people were going on about. I think she's absolutely beautiful and she's so cool.

JESY: I remember the first time I saw something. I was watching one of our videos on YouTube and I didn't realise that you could comment on them. I scrolled down and saw some comments and one said, 'The girl on the right is a right fat b***h.' The other girls told me to ignore it, but then I started reading more and they were all saying the same thing. All the girls were telling me to ignore them, but I kept reading more and more. My mum had asked me before I went into the show if I'd be able to handle it if people said negative things and I'd said, 'Of course, it comes with the territory. I'll be fine. You'll always get people like that who say things.' But then you see it in black and white ... I didn't understand why people were taking time out to be so nasty. Sometimes people would take a picture of us as a band and cut me out and replace me with a picture of a really fat person or an alien. I was crying at one point and saying I wanted to go home because of how much it affected me. People were telling me not to let other people ruin my experience, but it was so hurtful. I didn't want to do choreography or go into the studio because I felt so down. I became obsessed with what people were saying and wanted to cry all the time. Even though I knew it would hurt me, I kept reading. I have no idea why. I know that Marcus got a hard time as well, and he and I talked about it together. Now I don't read any comments because you can read a hundred nice comments and it's the one nasty one that gets to you. On the positive side I did also get so much support from people.

PERRIE: People were saying quite rightly how awful it was, and what total and utter rubbish.

JESY: For a while I felt like that's all I'd become known for. If I was walking down the street I'd start to think, 'The only reason you know me is because of the bullying.' Some people became even worse when they knew how much it upset me, but some people really got behind me and sent me lovely messages. A lot of girls came up to me and said that they'd been bullied and that I'd really helped them to get over it as well, so that was very touching. Everything horrible has an upside. As much as I hated it all being shown on telly, I'm glad it helped some people.

JADE: It wasn't easy for Jesy to talk about it on camera, and I was so proud of her when she did. I think it helped people to understand how she was feeling and just how much damage can be done when people write such unpleasant things. That they are read by people, so you should be mindful of what you say. People need to put themselves into the other person's shoes and imagine how hurtful it can be. Just because someone is in the public eye, it doesn't mean things don't affect them the same as they affect other people.

PERRIE: Anyone who meets Jesy can see how amazing she is. She's perfect as she is. I tried my hardest not to bite back at people who wrote nasty things about anyone, but I read this one ridiculous comment about Jesy and I couldn't help myself. I wrote on Twitter, 'You must have a lot of issues if you have to sit behind a laptop and say these things from behind a screen. #growapair.' I didn't say anything too mean, but our fans joined in and defended Jesy. They were amazing about it all.

JESY: The funny thing is that I did put on weight in *X Factor* because we were eating so much and grabbing what we could, and it was always fatty foods. We were so tired and we had no energy, so we'd just eat, and we had no time to exercise. Then when I left the show I got back into my normal routine of eating sensibly, and everyone started saying that I'd been on a diet and had a personal trainer. It was so ridiculous. One report said I ate porridge for breakfast every morning, and another one said I was working out for three hours a day. As if! Loads of people put on weight in *The X Factor* and then lose it when they come out. People are so obsessed with weight and it's so unfair. You get slammed if you're too thin and slammed if you're curvy. I just don't want girls to get influenced by the negativity. Everyone should be allowed to feel good about themselves. I will admit that I got obsessed with how I looked during the show, because I was in magazines or newspapers every day with comments about my appearance. But since then I've had so much going on that I've forgotten about it all and realised that it's not that much of a big deal. There were some photos of me on holiday in a

bikini in the press a while ago, and while I'd rather they hadn't been printed, I managed to shrug it off. I've learnt to stop caring what other people think. I'm happy in the way I look now. I want to be able to go on holiday and enjoy it and wear a bikini without worrying. I got nice feedback from it as well, so it was really cool.

LEIGH-ANNE: We've all got comments on Twitter but we've learnt to ignore the negativity. If us being true to who we are helps one girl who has low self-esteem, then that's brilliant. We're happy to show our flaws and be open about them.

PERRIE: Some people said on Twitter that I looked like Pat Butcher and I just

laughed. I was at an awards show and my hair was up and I was wearing these massive earrings, so they came up with that comparison. It's hilarious. Everyone is going to have an opinion. I'm more annoyed when people say things about the other girls than when something mean is said about me. People have opinions about us now – so be it.

JADE: We were excited from the moment we chose our song for Halloween week. It was our favourite song so far and we wanted everyone else to love it. It was quite scary, as we had a few tricks

----

BELOW: Leigh-Anne getting ready to go out

up our sleeves and we were taking some chances, but why not?

JESY: We went all out with our costumes and make-up and made it as extreme as it could be. We wanted it to be crazy. It was Halloween after all, so we had to embrace it!

LEIGH-ANNE: We sat on swings with our faces painted like dolls, singing Katy's Perry's 'E.T.' It was the first time we'd stayed so still! But then we got up and did a bit of a dance routine too.

PERRIE: When Kelly was ill, Alexandra Burke stood in for her on the judging panel, and she was so nice to us. She said we'd upped the levels for groups on the show and that we had massive potential. Gary praised our voices, and admitted that he couldn't pick a winner, which we took to mean we could be in the running. How exciting! Louis also said we were four of the nicest girls he'd ever met, and he was so sweet when he told Jesy not to worry about the things people had been saying because they're just jealous.

JESY: Tulisa said she was proud of me for speaking out about my insecurities, and I was so touched that I started crying on stage again. It was just such a lovely thing to say, and all of the judges made me feel better about everything. Going through something like that and hearing other people talk about their hang-ups just shows how many of us don't feel good enough about ourselves, and for no good reason.

JADE: We enjoyed the performance so much and I loved the fact that we looked a bit creepy. Although it's probably not a good everyday look.

PERRIE: I was buzzing by the time we came off stage. I think it was my favourite of all our performances up until that point.

JADE: By the time Sunday even came around we were a bag of nerves again, praying that we wouldn't get sent home. We'd had such a crazy week and we were desperate to get through and break the girl-band curse. Belle Ami had gone out in Week 4 the year before, and we didn't want to go the same way.

JESY: When we made it through we were all high-fiving each other backstage because we had officially broken the curse of the girl bands! We were properly happy.

LEIGH-ANNE: We felt like we had loads more to offer, so we wanted to be able to come back week after week and show that.

PERRIE: We wanted people to be surprised every time we went out on stage. The last thing we wanted was to be predictable.

GIRL
BANDS
CAN

JESY: Week 5 was such a laugh, and for some reason it made us all even closer. I guess, because of the name change and all the things that had happened the week before, we'd bonded more than ever.

LEIGH-ANNE: The brilliant thing about us is that we're all happy to do our own thing as well. We're not glued to each other's sides. Sometimes we are together 24 hours a day and we were totally happy about it, but if a couple of us wanted to go off and do something or someone wanted some alone time, no one got funny about it. We all give each other space, and we can tell if one of the other girls wants to take five minutes away to chill out and be by herself. We can read each other very well.

PERRIE: We can sense immediately if someone is tired or feeling a bit rubbish. We give them time out, but we also comfort them if they want it. There were times during the competition when we were so tired we didn't know what do with ourselves. But I don't want that to sound like I'm moaning, because I'm not at all. Every single second was worth it.

JADE: We got run down and ill at different stages, but if someone was feeling a bit under the weather we'd lift them back up again. I know that people think it's really unusual because we're all girls, but there really isn't any bitchiness between us.

JESY: We were ridiculously lucky this week because we got to go and see Jessie J in concert. We were so excited to see her again, because obviously she was the one who put us through to the live shows in Greece, along with Tulisa. When we were walking through the audience people were recognising us, which was mad.

LEIGH-ANNE: During the gig we got up on stage with Jessie J and helped her to sing 'Price Tag'. How mad is that? The crowd were amazing and it gave us a taste of what life could be like for us in the future if we worked hard.

JADE: We were not even supposed to go on, but we saw The Risk go up and we were like 'That's not fair!' So we ran on too and it was the craziest thing.

PERRIE: I was like a rabbit caught in the headlights. I didn't know where to look. We were dancing like absolute idiots and the crowd were screaming.

LEIGH-ANNE: Jessie J is such an inspiration, I was asking the girls to pinch me because I couldn't actually believe we'd just been on stage with her. Things like that just don't happen!

JADE: That week we also recorded the *X Factor* charity single, a cover of 'When You Wish upon a Star'. That was another amazing experience.

PERRIE: All the proceeds from sales went to an incredible charity called Together for Short Lives, which provides care and support for young people who tragically aren't expected to live long enough to reach adulthood.

JESY: It meant so much to us to be asked to take part, and we were so

touched when we heard some of the stories and met some of the people involved with the charity. It made what we've been doing for the past five weeks mean so much more. It's easy to forget where you are while you're in the show, because there's so much going on around you, and when we went out to film the video it made me realise how big what we were doing was and what a difference it would make to these kids' lives.

LEIGH-ANNE: It was wicked knowing we were doing something for such a good cause. It was amazing going to the hospice and seeing all of the children. I'm a very emotional person, so I was in tears at times, but it felt incredible to know that we were in a position where we could genuinely help.

JADE: It was just such a lovely thing to be able to do. We had loads of fake snow and it was the first time we met JLS and One Direction. The single went to number one as well, which was incredible. We hope it raised loads and loads of money.

JESY: Tulisa said that she wanted us to push things even more in Week 5. She wanted us to take things a step further and blow everyone out of the water. She knows what she's talking about and we trusted her every step of the way – and we loved what she suggested for us.

JADE: The theme was Dancefloor Fillers, and we sang Rihanna's 'Please Don't Stop the Music' mashed up with Michael Jackson's 'Wanna Be Startin' Something'. We wore these mad metallic outfits and had jewels on our faces.

JESY: Louis said he loved everything about our performance and that we were going to be in the show for a long time, and Kelly said she believed in us but she wanted us to do something a cappella.

PERRIE: Gary said he loved the fact we'd raided Johnny Robinson's wardrobe, which I thought was dead funny.

LEIGH-ANNE: The Sunday elimination was scarier than any other week because it was a double elimination. We were really worried, but we prayed that people would pick up the phone and vote for us.

JESY: When we found out we'd got through and The Risk were going home we were gobsmacked. We never thought we would be the last band standing.

LEIGH-ANNE: Losing The Risk that week was awful. Tulisa looked so sad, bless her. The groups were so close and we'd all made the journey together. Ashford and I were even in the same group at Bootcamp, and then he left the competition with Nu Vibe – and now he was gone again. I couldn't stop crying. I knew how much he wanted it and deserved it, and I felt so guilty that I was still in the show and he wasn't.

JESY: I missed Ashford the most too. He was always the one who was up early cracking jokes, and he was so lovely to be around.

PERRIE: We were so stunned when their name was called. Everyone was. We were in tears backstage and it proved beyond doubt that no one in the competition was safe, because we thought they would be there right until the final week. Now we were Tulisa's last remaining act and we could not let her down.

JESY: After The Risk went out, the house started to feel really empty and different from the place that we'd been living in. We felt like we were rattling around a bit. But then four of the acts who had already left the competition came back to fight for their chance to go back in, so it suddenly filled up again.

LEIGH-ANNE: It got really lively again and felt as if we had started all over again. It was great to see everyone back, and the atmosphere got a lot more tense, but also exciting.

PERRIE: Tulisa invited us over to her house that week for dinner and made us curried goat. I'd never eaten it before but it was lovely, and we had a great girlie night in. It was fab to just gossip and play with her dogs! I shamed myself at the dinner table, though, because I kept burping. They showed it all on *Xtra Factor* and I was mortified.

JESY: We actually got to meet Lady Gaga when she was performing on the show, and she was so normal and lovely. We chatted to her for ages and it made me realise that celebrities are just like the rest of us. It was incredible meeting her, because she's a proper superstar and so talented. She was really inspirational.

JADE: We always worked really hard throughout the competition, but we knew that for that Saturday's show we needed to take it up another notch.

JESY: We rehearsed all week and we put everything into it, and when it came to the daytime rehearsals on the Saturday I suddenly felt completely and utterly exhausted. It all got too much for me and I started crying, but Tulisa comforted me. I think we were putting so much pressure on ourselves that I just cracked. But Tulisa was always there to make us feel better and confident that we could do it. And on the night, it was so fantastic.

JADE: I think there were just some times where we were so exhausted that we didn't know how we would make it through another performance.

LEIGH-ANNE: It was overwhelming sometimes. I once rang my mum and just started crying, and once I started I couldn't stop. It helped us to get everything out when we got upset, so we didn't give ourselves a hard time about it.

PERRIE: In honour of Queen and Lady Gaga week we did a mash-up of Lady Gaga's 'Telephone' and Queen's 'Radio Ga Ga'.

LEIGH-ANNE: Louis said that Little Mix had a big future, but Gary said we were a little bit predictable, so we made a decision to sing a ballad if we got through to the next week.

JESY: We kind of expected Gary to say that, because we did have a slow song but it got changed at the last minute, so maybe that's what people were expecting from us. But quite a few acts did slow songs, so it was nice for people to have an act they could have fun with and dance along to.

JADE: We had a great time up on stage and we did take Gary's comments on board, but we also hoped that they wouldn't affect the way people were going to vote.

PERRIE: We were down to the last three acts, and when our name was called out my heart was racing. I thought I was going to pass out. In the end Kitty got voted out, and she was such a character that she was definitely missed around the house.

JADE: Amelia Lily was voted back in, which was something we were all really happy about. She's a brilliant performer and I don't think she deserved to go out in the first week. It was more pressure on us, as it was a bit more competition, but it just meant that we would try even harder.

JESY: Week 7 was the most full-on but incredible week we'd had so far. When you're in a girl group it's pretty much non-stop, and those seven days were no exception.

PERRIE: It's all go, go, go, and you're constantly learning new things. We got to meet The Saturdays that week, which was amazing as we're big fans, and they gave us some great advice.

WE'RE LIVING THE DREAM

LEIGH-ANNE: They are so cool and properly nice. They were really friendly to us. Una told us that the most important thing about being in a girl band is friendship, and she said that she could tell that we all got on really well.

PERRIE: Mollie said that she could tell instantly that we were genuine friends, which meant a lot to us. Vanessa also said that looking at us reminded them of how they were when they first started out, which we took as a massive compliment. We really look up to other girl bands – in fact, more than ever now that we know how much hard work and dedication is involved. Rochelle said that the girls were rooting for us and they couldn't wait to have another girl band on the scene with them.

JADE: Meeting The Saturdays made us realise that all of the hard work does pay off and it can bring about amazing things. We were like 'We can make it!' I'd love loads of girls to look up to us the way they do to them. To think we could be the next Spice Girls or Saturdays or Girls Aloud is so crazy. People tell us they can see dolls being made of us already, and I'd love that. How cool would it be to have a mini version of yourself?

JESY: That week we got to go to the premiere of *Twilight: Breaking Dawn*. We walked up the red carpet and had our photo taken and got asked for autographs. We couldn't believe how loud it was. The fans there were just incredible. I was trying to be all professional but I kept getting distracted by seeing so many famous people. They were literally everywhere.

PERRIE: Taylor Lautner was interviewed by one of the *X Factor* camera crews and he sent us good luck wishes. How insane is that? Taylor Lautner knows who we are!

JESY: We loved every minute of it, and having a peek at that world made us want it even more. Imagine going to premieres every week! It would be like a dream.

PERRIE: If that kind of thing does happen to us, the good thing is that we're not the kind of girls who will go off the rails. I don't drink, I've never smoked a cigarette in my life and drugs are a no-go area. We aren't mad party girls at all. We all like to go out and have fun, but we're not going to get sucked into the party scene – the band means far too much to us for that. We all like to have a cheeky glass of wine now and again, but who doesn't?

LEIGH-ANNE: This week we were determined to show Gary Barlow that we weren't predictable. We took ages choosing the perfect song and we wanted it to be all about the vocals.

JADE: For Movie Week we performed En Vogue's 'Don't Let Go', which is such a classic track and featured in the film *Set It Off*.

PERRIE: I really liked our outfits that week. We were in black and white and looked quite smart. It was different to anything we'd worn before.

JESY: After we sang, Kelly said that we'd done everything she'd been hoping for in terms of how we looked and the vocals. She hadn't been critical of us in the past, but she said she wanted to see us showcasing our voices more, which the song did.

PERRIE: She said we could be the best girl group to come out of the UK, and Gary said he thought it was our best performance to date. Then Louis said we were 'ready-made pop stars' – amazing! Tulisa said she was really proud of us, which was the icing on the cake.

JADE: Sunday was both brilliant and terrifying, because we knew there was a chance we could go, which was awful. But Rihanna was appearing on the show, which we were all beside ourselves about. That really lifted our spirits.

LEIGH-ANNE: I was desperate to sort out a meeting with Rihanna, but I didn't have a clue what to say to her. I thought I'd just end up gawping and being really star-struck. Her management said that no one could meet her because she had loads to do, and I was gutted. Then I was standing at the entrance of the studio as she walked past, and she stopped and said to me, 'Your hair is awesome!' I literally couldn't believe it. It was amazing. I'll keep that with me forever.

JESY: We were really pleased with our performance the night before. It was so different to what we'd normally done, but we liked stepping out of our comfort zone. We were never going to be overly confident or think that we were safe at any point during the competition,

because no one is. But we really hoped that our fans were supporting us and would get us through. That's all we could hope for.

PERRIE: We were properly stunned when Craig got eliminated. He had such a brilliant voice and we all thought that he could win. He said backstage that he did feel like he might be going home that week, but he was still gutted.

JADE: So were we. He's such a great guy and we'd got really close to him.

LEIGH-ANNE: It was weird without him in the house. It was weird every time someone went, but we missed him loads. It was such a massive house and it felt bigger whenever people left.

JADE: The pressure was well and truly on in Week 8 because each act was performing two songs. Gary had told us he wanted to hear something that was more stripped back from us, so if there was ever a time do it, it was then.

PERRIE: We were quite tired that week, because we had two lots of vocal rehearsals and choreography, but we really enjoyed all of the rehearsals. We worked a lot with a guy called Eliot Kennedy, who is amazing. He taught us so much about how to harmonise and how to make our voices work best together. He was amazing to have around during the competition because he was so supportive and always there for us.

JADE: We got to have a lot of fun that week too, because we went to the opening of Winter Wonderland in Hyde Park. It was so Christmassy, and on the way there we were singing 'All I Want for Christmas Is You' in the back of the car.

JESY: Tulisa came with us, and we went on the bumper cars and on a giant slide. She also made us go on all of these really scary rides and we had so much fun. My mouth was aching afterwards because we'd been laughing so much.

PERRIE: It was really weird hearing people screaming our names. We were waving at everyone like mad. I was scared because I get very nervous about going on rides, but Tulisa is so persuasive she convinced me to go on all of them, and I loved them in the end.

JESY: We also got invited to appear on Radio One's *Surgery* programme and talk about issues that are affecting young people. I was asked about the comments that were made about me, and it felt so good to be able to say loud and proud that I'm not going to change myself because of them. I'm not going on a diet, I'm not going to try and be something I'm not. Your insecurities are what make you different and what make you who you are, and if everyone looked the same it would be boring! We're all different and I like being me. One girl said that seeing me go on stage looking happy and comfortable with who I am was inspiring to her, which felt so good. I also got sent some flowers during the show and the card read, 'To Jesy, the most beautiful girl I've ever

---

OPPOSITE: Jade picking out outfits

seen.' It was so touching. Things like that give you such a boost.

LEIGH-ANNE: The very funniest thing about Week 8 was that we went on speed dates with Jedward. Louis Walsh set it up – he was trying to get us together with them for a bit of a joke. It was absolutely hilarious. They even had a bell that they rang if the date was going badly.

JESY: I went first. They told me my hair was amazing and asked if my lip-gloss tasted as good as it looked. But then they rang the bell on me. How dare they!

JADE: I went second and asked them how they wear hoodies over their quiffs, and they rang the bell on me immediately just because of that. It definitely wasn't a match made in heaven.

LEIGH-ANNE: I went third and I asked what kind of cake they would make me if they could bake anything. They said they'd make me an ice-cream cake, because I'm so hot it would melt. It was seriously cheesy.

PERRIE: I was last and they offered to show me their muscles. I was in hysterics. They were such sweet guys and absolutely bonkers. You literally can't control them. They live in Jedward world.

JESY: Leigh-Anne and I were picked by the guys, but funnily enough the date hasn't happened. And I'm not sure it will be happening any time soon!

We were feeling so lucky and happy that we'd got so far in the competition, and as we were down to the final five we'd realised that we really could even win it.

LEIGH-ANNE: It was so weird to think that we had celebrity fans who were voting for us. The Saturdays, Davina McCall, Holly Willoughby, James Corden, Jermaine Defoe, David Walliams, One Direction, Mel C, Amelle from the Sugababes, Emma Bunton and Coleen and Wayne Rooney were all tweeting about us. It was so cool!

JESY: We chose our Week 8 songs the way we chose all of our other songs – very carefully! Just to make things that bit harder for ourselves we decided to do another mash-up of two tracks for our first performance – Justin Bieber's 'Baby' and The Supremes' 'Where Did Our Love Go?'

JADE: The theme was Musical Heroes. I grew up listening to Diana Ross, and for quite a while when I was younger I actually thought my mam *was* Diana Ross. I'm a massive fan. I absolutely adored her and still do to this day, so I really loved that performance.

PERRIE: We opened the show, which always feels weird, and our feedback was mixed. We were gutted because we knew how much was at stake, but it was all constructive criticism. Gary really enjoyed it, though, and said it was a great opening to the show.

JESY: For our second song we chose Christina Aguilera's 'Beautiful'.

JADE: It really was our hero song and is everything that Little Mix are about. Whenever I feel down I listen to that song and it makes me realise that everything is alright.

JESY: When I was singing that song it took me right back to being younger and how I felt about myself. I felt and meant every word I sang.

PERRIE: We all got really emotional, and by the end of the track we were all crying.

LEIGH-ANNE: I don't think we had ever felt closer singing a song together. It meant everything to us. The audience went mad when we finished and I can't describe how good that felt.

PERRIE: Louis said we pulled it out of the bag for the second song, and as soon as he said that I felt a real sense of relief. It would have been awful if a song that means so much to us hadn't had the effect we wanted it to. He also said he wanted to see us in the final. He wasn't the only one!

JESY: Kelly said that she wanted everyone to vote for us and she wanted to see us at the top of the charts. Then she told us we were all beautifully unique and when we come together it's something special. That set me off crying again!

JADE: Gary commented on how good our friendship was, and Tulisa said that it was our best performance to date.

JESY: I loved the fact that we got to show two sides of ourselves – our fun side and a really slow, emotional side. It was the first time we'd just sat there and sung like that with no dancing or anything. We knew it was still anyone's game, because everyone left in the competition was so good and working so hard.

LEIGH-ANNE: On the Sunday night we got to perform 'When You Wish upon a Star'. One Direction and JLS came along to the show to perform it with us. They're such nice guys, and they show just how far you can go after *The X Factor*.

JADE: The charity single was such a beautiful thing to do and we were really proud of it, so to be singing it in front of a big audience was wicked.

JADE: Although of course we were dead happy we stayed that week, we were gutted to say goodbye to Janet. She's a really sweet girl with a really unique voice.

LEIGH-ANNE: Jessie J performed on the show and it was so nice to catch up with her again. She gave us some good advice, which was to sing like no one's watching. That's something we carried on to the following week.

JESY: She also said to remember why we started out in the business – because we want to sing. I started crying and told her she was amazing. I couldn't hold myself back.

THE FINAL COUNT- DOWN

JADE: We went to another premiere in Week 9. It was for the film *Hugo*, and again it was wall-to-wall stars. We even saw Prince Charles and Camilla. Things like that just don't happen to girls like us and we were so, so grateful to be there.

PERRIE: I swear Prince Charles said he wanted us to win…

LEIGH-ANNE: People kept asking how we'd feel if we won, and it was such a surprise to realise that they all thought we had a good chance. We were asked to perform at the party afterwards, and that was just something else.

PERRIE: We sang En Vogue's 'Don't Let Go' and we felt like proper pop stars.

JESY: Everyone was dancing and singing along and I wanted to run into the crowd and hug everyone.

LEIGH-ANNE: We also did a secret gig at a Talk Talk store in Soho. It was a really small, intimate crowd, and Jeff Brazier was there with his two sons, who were so cute. We sang 'Don't Let Go' again and it went really well. It was so cool being in such a small space with fans, and it was great getting to meet them all. We went for some fast food afterwards on the way home because we'd worked up a bit of an appetite, so that was a nice treat.

PERRIE: One of my favourite moments of the week was when we went to M&S to shop for Christmas presents for our friends and family. We were unleashed

and running around the shop like mad women.

LEIGH-ANNE: I got my sister some amazing clothes for work. She'd been saying for a while that she wanted to add more colour to her work wardrobe and I think it gave her a lot more confidence. I got her a gorgeous gold cardigan, and the same chunky knit cardigan that I got given during the competition. It's so snug and lovely and I knew she'd like it.

JESY: I got myself some lovely black boots. You can never treat yourself too much, can you? I also got my mum two pairs of boots in black and brown, which she was so happy with.

JADE: My mission was to get my mam a coat, and I found the perfect one. I wanted to try and get my brother something, but men are so hard to choose for. In the end I found him a lovely cashmere jumper.

PERRIE: I must admit, the first thing I picked up was something for myself – a beanie hat with a bear's face on it. I did get some great presents as well, though, honest. We walked out of there with armfuls of stuff. It was such a treat. I wish I could do that every Christmas. My mum loved that Christmas because she got loads and loads of gifts. She deserves all the gifts in the world.

We were so excited to be in the semi-final. We reflected a lot around that time about how far we'd come and how much things had changed for us.

JESY: We'd all grown up a lot in the competition because we'd been away from our mums and we had to do everything for ourselves. We had to mature and learn to cook for ourselves. We didn't even know how to use a washing machine when we first went into the house.

LEIGH-ANNE: We didn't get any tidier over the weeks, though. I remember one of the *X Factor* crews coming round to film in our bedroom and it was so embarrassing. There were clothes everywhere and I think even they were shocked by how messy it was.

JADE: We never really had a chance to tidy up. We were rushing around so much that if we took something off we'd leave it on the floor. If we only have half an hour to get ready you can't expect to things to be neat as well! We could never find anything when we needed it, which was a bit of a problem.

LEIGH-ANNE: We all kept really grounded throughout. If anyone even thinks about having a diva moment the rest of us are there saying, 'Oi, what do you think you're doing?' We'll never get too big for our boots.

JESY: We really enjoyed performing in the semi-finals. We chose to sing The Supremes' 'You Keep Me Hanging On' and Beyoncé's 'If I Were a Boy'.

JADE: Louis said there was something missing when we sang 'You Keep Me Hanging On' and it was like we'd lost our mojo. He told us we'd need to pull it out of the bag for our second song.

PERRIE: Kelly said she'd seen us doing better vocal performances and expected more from us because we were so close to the final.

JESY: Gary told us he was a big fan but that we needed a lead singer.

PERRIE: He said I had the best voice, but that's not true. It was a lovely comment, but we all have our strengths and bring something different to the group and that's what makes us a team.

JESY: Tulisa didn't agree with Gary. She started arguing with him and Louis, saying we didn't need a lead singer.

JADE: We appreciated what they said and just hoped they'd like 'If I Were a Boy' better.

PERRIE: We loved how it went and had a massive cuddle afterwards. Louis said we had amazing potential and that we were the next big girl band. Yay!

JESY: Kelly said it was all about finding out how to bring out the best in each other, and if we could do that we could change the world.

JADE: Sadly Gary said we'd had a bad night, but he still asked people to vote for us. We knew we weren't perfect and we still had things to learn, but we could

only hope that people could see we were willing to do that.

LEIGH-ANNE: Tulisa was really passionate and was telling everyone to vote for us because we deserved to win.

JESY: Her plea worked, because we made it to the final. The final! We were going to Wembley! We were in tears when we found out, which isn't like us at all!

PERRIE: In the final week it was more hectic than ever. If we thought we'd worked hard before, it was nothing compared to this. We were doing photo shoots and interviews and TV shows, the lot. But it was so worth it. We were beyond excited about the final. We could not believe we'd made it all that way.

LEIGH-ANNE: Even though we were tired we kept jumping around really excitedly whenever we talked about it – which was all the time!

JESY: It was the most important week in the competition, so deciding which songs to sing was scarier than it had ever been. We had to choose songs that would showcase our voices, let us put our stamp on them, and blow everyone away. After about a million discussions we decided on Candy Staton's 'You Got the Love' and a mash-up of Alicia Keys's 'If I Ain't Got You' and Jay-Z's 'Empire State of Mind', which we sang with Tulisa.

BELOW: Sneaking a five-minute kip on a shoot

JADE: We were such perfectionists; we always wanted to rehearse more. But there was so much to do, so we didn't get to properly rehearse until the Saturday. Every time we went to go and practise, one of the other girls would have been lured away to do an interview or something. I think the only time we were together all weekend was the time we spent on stage.

PERRIE: We were so nervous back-stage before the show at Wembley. We'd got used to the backstage area of the *X Factor* studios, and this was totally different, so it was a bit strange. We did get a great dressing-room, though.

JADE: We all helped each other stay calm before the show. One minute during the day we'd be screaming, and the next we'd be sitting there quietly feeling dead nervous. It was such a rollercoaster of emotions.

JESY: Stepping out on stage for the first time in the final at Wembley was just surreal. Usually artists have to wait years before they get to play Wembley, and we'd only been together for a matter of months – and there we were. It was so massive and I didn't know where to look. It was like a giant sea of faces. I know we've said it before, but we just didn't expect to be there for that long, and every week was a bonus, so to be there in the final week ... The audience were amazing and all of our performances went really well.

BELOW: Leaving for The Brits

Performing with Tulisa was incredible because even though she was our mentor, she was like our sister as well. She honestly doesn't realise how good she is though. She's so amazing.

JADE: We were so determined to go out there and smash our tracks and have an amazing time.

LEIGH-ANNE: We had the best time ever belting out our songs, and when we found out we'd got through to the grand final we were speechless. For once!

JADE: I don't think any of us slept properly that night – we were so excited and overwhelmed.

LEIGH-ANNE: It was the most ridiculous feeling when Sunday night came. We'd chosen our songs, En Vogue's 'Don't Let Go', 'Silent Night' and, of course, the winner's song, 'Cannonball'. We were really happy with what we'd picked, but it was all down to how it went on the night. We wanted to win so badly. Everything we'd done had been leading up to that moment. We'd made it to the final of *The X Factor*. It was a dream come true.

PERRIE: There we were, being given the chance to win *The X Factor*. Obviously a girl group had never won, so the thought that we could be the first was mind-blowing.

LEIGH-ANNE: We all enjoyed every minute of being up there. We did our very best and put everything into it.

JADE: We were so determined to enjoy it, so we went for it. But standing on the stage waiting to hear the results was the scariest moment of my life. Looking back I don't even remember much about it, except that my heart felt as if it was jumping out of my chest.

PERRIE: My legs were trembling. To know that this was the moment that could decide our future was so weird.

JESY: I honestly don't know how we managed to stand up there, because we were all shaking. The pressure was incredible and I was convinced that Marcus was going to win. I was looking at Dermot waiting for him to say Marcus's name, and then he paused for so, so long.

LEIGH-ANNE: I felt like we were on stage for about an hour, and yet things were going in slow motion. I just wanted to hear Dermot say our name more than anything I've ever wanted in my life.

OH MY GOODNESS! WE WOOOON!

JESY: I still can't believe it. Honestly. I just remember Tulisa hugging us on stage. We were all in a total daze.

LEIGH-ANNE: We were in total and utter shock – and we still are. Even now I think, 'Is this real? Is this really happening?' Everything that I've ever wanted to happen in my life has come true. Not many people can say that. It just shows that if you want something that badly you've got to go for it, because you just never know. If you work for it and you're determined and you believe, you can have it all.

PERRIE: It just hasn't sunk in at all that we won *The X Factor*. It's the most incredible thing ever.

JADE: Knowing we'd won was the best feeling in the world. At that moment, more than anything, we all wanted to hug our parents, and say thank you for everything they've ever done for us. We missed them so much during the competition. I remember watching Matt Cardle win, thinking he must have been buzzing, but when it actually happens to you, it's like a massive blur.

JESY: We just want to say thanks so much to everyone for your incredible support. We couldn't have done any of this without you and it means everything to us to know that you're there. Little Mix are here to stay!

JADE: Tulisa was the best mentor in the world. Not only was she incredible to work with but she was also our friend and always there for us. When she started crying when we won it set me off because I was so happy we'd made her so proud.

LEIGH-ANNE: We didn't get to party and celebrate after the show, but we didn't mind at all. We had to be up at four the following morning to be on *Daybreak* and then *This Morning*, and we wanted to be totally professional and start as we meant to go on. We've managed to celebrate since, but there's a time and a place, and late at night before an early TV appearance was not the time!

OPPOSITE: A final hug from our manager to wish us luck before we go on stage

JESY: We literally went to sleep and woke up buzzing. I woke up and said to Leigh-Anne, 'Did we really win *The X Factor* last night?' It took a while to get used to it. Winners' week was so crazy. It was constant interviews and going to radio stations and all sorts.

LEIGH-ANNE: It was a lot of late nights and early mornings, so it wasn't particularly glamorous, but we didn't mind at all. We filmed the *Top of the Pops* Christmas special, which was a dream. We'd all watched it as kids, so to be on it was madness. We didn't stop going for a second, but we had a break to look forward to, so that kept us going no matter how tired we were.

PERRIE: The day after we won was one of the funniest days of my life. We were like zombies, but we were on such a high that we kept going on adrenaline. In the late afternoon we had to do a load of internet interviews, and we were almost delirious with tiredness. We were that shattered that we got a bit hysterical, and everything was somehow absolutely hilarious. We were drinking sugary drinks and eating sweets, so we were totally hyperactive. I think the interviewers who came in were a little bit scared of us. We started getting a bit fruit loopy and we were apologising for being so crazy. Our management team were in hysterics because we were being so mad. I don't think we stopped laughing the whole time. My bed has never felt better than it did that night.

3. LIFE AFTER X FACTOR

CRACK-ING CHRIST-MAS

LEIGH-ANNE: Getting to go home the following week and to be with my family and see how proud they were was just incredible. It was the best Christmas I've ever had. Watching us on *Top of the Pops* on Christmas Day was so lovely. My family and friends treated me just the same as they always have, but it was strange walking down the street and being recognised. We had been in a big bubble in *The X Factor*, and it was only when I stepped outside of it that it hit me. Everyone wants a piece of you.

I'm a party girl so I went out a lot over Christmas. It's mad that when you get famous you can get into clubs and get drinks for free. I loved it! I went to a club in Watford with my friends and we got in the queue, and for a laugh one of my friends decided to go and tell the people on the door who I was. The next thing I know they let us straight in and gave us a table with sparklers and everything. It was such a fun night. My friends loved it too. It's so nice being able to treat them.

We all kept in touch with each other loads over Christmas and really missed each other. On New Year's Eve I met up with Jesy. We went to Mahiki in London with lots of our friends, and we had our own little section with a shower and bed and everything. It was crazy.

PERRIE: It was so nice going home and having a breather with my family over Christmas. My mum had recorded all of the *X Factor* shows, so we sat and watched them together. I was creasing up watching them. I felt on top of the world. I went shopping and bought lovely Christmas presents for my family and friends. I got my mum a new car and my brother an Apple laptop. They were well pleased! I love being able to buy them presents, it feels amazing. I've got everything I need, so if I'm shopping I make sure I get them things too.

I didn't get recognised a lot over Christmas, even though I was out loads. I think unless someone is a die-hard Little Mix fan they wouldn't look twice at me. I'm just a little blonde girl, whereas Jesy has the amazing style and the hair, so everyone knows who she is! But then as soon as one person recognises you, others do and you end up with a bit of a queue. There was one time over Christmas when my mum and I were out shopping and as we were walking along, these girls were whispering, 'Is that Perrie from Little Mix?' My mum turned round and said, 'It is! Do you want a picture?' She was so proud of me.

My entire family were so proud of me. My stepmum Joanne is so supportive and excited for me, and my dad says that sometimes he's driving down the road and all of a sudden he'll start smiling because he's so excited for me. My little 11-year-old stepsister Caitlin loves it all as well. She's dead mature for her age and she's taking it all really well, even though all of her friends at school keep asking about us. She even used to ask permission to get our autograph. She's so cute. I love her to pieces, I call her my baba. Hanging out with her and chatting and watching *Art Attack* is what keeps me grounded.

I went out with my brother for New Year. We went to Weymouth and everyone was dressing up, so my brother and I went as punk rockers. My cousin Kelsie was only out for a few hours because she's

pregnant, but after she went everyone else started getting into the booze. Mum and I don't drink, so as soon as everyone started getting really drunk we sneaked off to the kebab shop and got pizza, chips and curry sauce and went home. We didn't even tell anyone we were going, we just slipped out.

I've never been a drinker. I drank once on holiday when I was 15. My best friend at the time, Jasmine, and I got properly drunk, and when I went to bed the room was spinning. When I woke up the next day I was so hungover and felt incredibly sick. I've hardly ever drunk since. I'll have a cheeky glass of wine every now and again with my dinner, but getting drunk was the worst experience of my life. I never want to feel like that again. That taught me a lesson!

JESY: Going back home and getting to spend time with my family was amazing. It sounds silly, but it was nice to be normal again. It was so weird when my mum and I went out shopping. I'm so used to being able to just pop to the shops and I love it, but I hadn't done it since being in the show. We went to Lakeside Shopping Centre and I couldn't even get out of one shop because there was a swarm of people outside. In the end I had to get some security guards to help me. I literally went to two shops and then left again because it was so mad. I had dyed my hair red by then, which I thought would help as I was known for my big blonde hair, but if anything it was worse. I guess it drew a lot of attention.

I slept loads over Christmas. It was so nice to go to bed and know I didn't have to be up at 4am. I think my family really liked spending time with me, because

they knew that come New Year I would be away loads, working.

I was with Leigh-Anne for New Year's Eve. We both took all of our friends to Mahiki and it was a good laugh. It was a nice way to see in 2012. In fact I'm not a massive clubber. Leigh-Anne and Jade are party girls, but I'd rather go to the cinema. Perrie and I are much more the kind to cosy up on the sofa, but I really enjoyed it.

JADE: Christmas was a magical time for all of us. We only had about two weeks off, and it went too quickly, but I managed to fit a lot in. I had a proper big Christmas dinner with my family, and then on Boxing Day I had a birthday party so I could catch up with everyone.

Sadly I really didn't enjoy it much. I spent most of the night having photos taken with people, and they were queuing up to speak to me. It was weird because these were my friends that I'd known for years. I felt like I was doing a signing, not having a birthday party.

That was a big lesson for me. It wasn't really their fault, but I ended the night crying because it hit me that things have changed so much. I'm not just a friend to those people any more, but somebody they know who is famous.

On New Year's Eve I went to a house party with some of my best friends. I knew I might not have much of a chance to do that again for a while, so we went along and relived some of the old times and properly caught up with Holly, Anna and Sarah, which was so lovely.

NEW YEAR, NEW LIFE

JESY: We all got back together again just after New Year and we were thrown straight back into work. We didn't have a permanent place to stay, so we were living in hotels, and it was great being back together. It was so exciting to be back at work. We were totally ready for it after our break.

We knew we wanted to get our music out quite quickly after leaving *The X Factor*, so we were aware that we would be working quite intensely. We'd got a good taste of being in the studios while we were doing the show, but it was nothing compared to working on our own music. We were a bit worried because we had such high expectations of what we wanted our single to sound like. It was really different from anything else out there, so we were praying that people would get it. I got goose bumps when TMS played us this particular backing track. Our A&R lady, Anya, had said to us that when you hear your first single, you just know. And that's how it was for us in that moment.

We've got a lot to say and we're on the same wavelength, so we love sitting around and writing together.

I'll never forget going to meet Simon. I felt like I was meeting the Queen, but he was the loveliest guy. I've always had a little bit of a crush on him anyway, and I had been so gutted when we heard he wasn't going to be a judge on the show. We were all sitting there in awe of him. I couldn't believe I was sitting having a casual chat with Simon Cowell in his office! He told us he loved our first single, 'Wings', and that he was really excited about it. To hear that from him was pretty exciting for us too! We were definitely a bit star-struck.

JADE: I knew I would miss everyone from home when I left, but I also couldn't wait to get back to work and make a start on everything. I really missed the girls over Christmas, because we'd spent every day with each other for four months. We talked loads on the phone, but it was so nice to see them all again. We had some meetings about what was going to happen next and got our heads around everything that was coming up. It was exciting – there was so much to look forward to.

Going into the studio again was also exciting, because we were working on our own music and being really creative. And you get to eat nice food in studios! Perrie and I love curry, but Jesy and Leigh-Anne were being really healthy so we tried to follow their lead. I get tired if I eat too much junk food, so I try to eat as well as possible, but when there's curry on offer …

A song is not a Little Mix song unless we're putting our stamp on it, so we made sure that we got our opinion across with everything – in a good way! Of course we're working with incredible people too and we're learning so much from them, but we do have very firm ideas. We don't want to do songs that are just about going to a club and partying and getting drunk. We want there to be more to it than that, and we want to have some really nice, strong messages.

I was in total shock when we got to go and meet Simon Cowell. I'd met him before when I'd auditioned, but this was going to his office and hanging out with him so it was a totally different situation. He said he'd always wanted to have a successful girl band and that he saw massive potential in us. You know you're doing something right if Simon likes you!

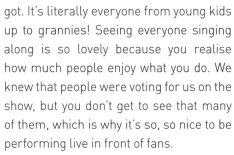

LEIGH-ANNE: After Christmas we did some gigs and played at some private parties, which was really great. We all loved performing at GAY. The crowd was incredible and it was such a laugh. It's amazing how much more relaxed we felt being out of the *X Factor* house. Whenever we performed on the show we were being evaluated, so it was so nice to get on stage and sing and not worry about being judged and criticised. We could just get out on stage and do what we loved.

We got to see loads of our supporters and we realised what a wide fan base we've got. It's literally everyone from young kids up to grannies! Seeing everyone singing along is so lovely because you realise how much people enjoy what you do. We knew that people were voting for us on the show, but you don't get to see that many of them, which is why it's so, so nice to be performing live in front of fans.

When we were back in the studio it was like 'Okay, we're pop stars now. We're in the studio recording and writing with amazing producers.' We worked with Andrea Martin, who wrote En Vogue's 'Don't Let Go'; Autumn Row, who's written for Leona Lewis and Cher Lloyd; Steve Mac and Biff, who have worked with everyone, and TMS. They're amazing, and they're our boys. They wrote 'No Regrets' for Dappy and 'Read All About It' for Emeli Sandé.

We know exactly what we want our sound to be like, and when we hear it we just know if it works. It's not like one of us likes something and the others don't – we all have the same view on it. Writing together is brilliant as well, because it comes from us and from our hearts. Our A&R people and Simon Cowell said that our best work would come from us, and they're so right because we really feel it.

We're mixing pop, R&B and hip-hop all in one. We want to have that cool sound and that edge. We're not a typical pop girl group. We want to be uplifting and sing about things that people can relate to and get something from. We want to be inspirational.

We went to Simon Cowell's offices to meet up with him and talk about our music

OPPOSITE: One of Jade's boxes of bow ties

and our future and it felt surreal. He's so nice and just like he is on TV. He's got really high hopes for us and we're going to do everything we can to go all the way.

❋ **PERRIE:** Being back in London was cool, but I think we did miss our families initially. You take for granted how much they do for you, like all of the cooking and cleaning and just being there to give you a hug, so to be in a hotel room on your own can feel strange. We loved being back together, though. We'd missed each other loads. We see our families as much as we can and we're always on the phone to them.

We loved, loved, loved being back in the studio too, and we were so pleased with how everything went. We worked with some incredible people and spent ages listening to different tracks and putting lyrics together, but when we heard our first single we just knew it was right. It was like being hit by lightning. We all looked at each other and that was it. We talked about releasing our own music so many times when we were taking part in *The X Factor*, and now that it was actually happening we were all beside ourselves with happiness. But it had to be perfect.

If we're going to be singing something for the rest of our lives it has to come from us, which is why we're so involved in the writing and the whole of the creative process. We're not bossy, but we've got strong ideas. I think that's one of the things Simon Cowell likes about us actually. The meeting with him went so well, and I think he already knew that we were strong girls and we knew what we wanted.

YOU WANT SOMETHING THAT BADLY YOU'VE GOT TO GO FOR IT

ROAD MIXERS

JESY: We were so excited about going out on the road with the tour. It was one of things we talked about most when we were in the show. We loved doing tour rehearsals, because we got to meet up with all of the other acts again. Everyone was so relaxed because there was no competition, and we got on really well. Doing rehearsals and knowing that you're going to be performing to thousands was lovely. We met the dancers we were going to be working with, and I loved every minute of learning the routines. Flying around the stadiums too – that's something you don't usually get to do unless you're Beyoncé or Rihanna, so we felt really lucky when we found out we were doing it.

Touring was the best experience ever. There was no pressure. We were just going out on stage and having fun – and getting a bit of spare time to shop! The best feeling is being on stage and seeing a little girl in a Little Mix t-shirt with a Little Mix banner, singing and dancing along to our music. And I loved it when there were grown-up couples and the boyfriend would be singing and dancing along too and having a brilliant time. There is no better feeling than singing live on stage. The fans are the whole reason we're here, so it feels really good to be able to say thank you to them.

We had a few good aftershow parties too. It was funny if we all went out in a big group, because people would stare and be like 'What are they doing here?' I felt so sad when it was all over. I really missed being around everyone, but we're going to stay in touch with them all.

LEIGH-ANNE: When we saw the things we were getting to do on tour, like flying and the dance break in 'Super Bass', we were so happy. Beth and Nicky, the choreographers, were amazing.

Styling for the tour was quite hard because we've all got our own individual styles, which we needed to merge, but we managed to get there. We can't wait to do our own tour and go all out with our costumes, because I know we'll really push things. The first show was a matinee, so it wasn't that crazy, but the evening show was absolutely mad. We popped up at the beginning of our set from these things called 'toasters', which spring you up into the air. We used to stand on stage listening to the VT of our journey on the show and I got a real rush listening to it and seeing how far we'd come.

I think the tour was a real taste of what's to come in the future. Performing to arenas every night is surreal. It's such a buzz knowing that the reason you're on stage is that everyone loves you and appreciates what you're doing.

We hung out with Craig and Marcus loads, and also The Risk, and we had a few good nights out. I made sure I looked after myself, though, and I was keeping my strength up by going to the gym as well.

I ate as healthily as I could. I had put on so much weight when I was doing *The X Factor* and I really hated it. I lost it after I left the show because then I was running, but on the tour we were eating so much backstage and having junk food so it just went on again. We were eating a fry-up for breakfast and then used to have two more three-course meals. It was a bit ridiculous. When I'm on TV I get really self-conscious about it showing in my face, as that's where the weight seems to go on.

I'm eating really healthily now, which I enjoy, and I also exercise whenever I can.

✱ PERRIE: We were so full of energy and ready for the tour. I loved being able to get fit while we were doing the rehearsals, because it was a fun way to do it. We put in long hours as we always do, but it was such a laugh as well. All of the dancers were so cool and I learnt loads of new steps.

Nothing compares to touring. The audiences in Dublin were insane, and I was properly welling up when we played Newcastle. It was so sweet being home, and all my friends and family came along. We shopped everywhere we went, and I had to buy a new massive pink suitcase to get all of my stuff in.

It was amazing travelling around the country. A lot of the places we visited I was seeing for the first time, so that was cool. And of course we got to meet loads of the fans, which was wicked. It was so nice getting a proper chance to catch up with so many people. As for the fans, they've been unbelievable. To be able to see them all and say thanks was the best thing. They're the ones that have got us here and we can never say just how grateful we are.

⋈ JADE: We did laugh a lot during tour rehearsals. We'd never done anything like the amazing tricks and flying we were doing, so we got a bit giddy sometimes. We were rehearsing at the place where JLS were practising for their tour, so we kept bumping into them. They were dead sweet to us and telling us how amazing it is being on the road.

Travelling to many different places was wicked. I was crying in Newcastle. It was so emotional for Perrie and me being back in our home town.

We used to get warmed up backstage by putting on some music and jumping around madly. Then, just before we went on, Kitty would be performing 'Edge of Glory', so we'd do some more dancing and that would get us in the mood. It affects your performance if you're feeling tired or down, so we always got ourselves pumped up and ready to go.

At every venue we used to get crisps, drinks, fruit and a box of sweets in our dressing-room, so that was always really tempting. The only things we actually asked for were water and bananas to give us energy. We weren't exactly demanding!

We had a real laugh hanging out on the tour bus. Quite often we'd listen to music and jam together or watch DVDs, and to pass the time we used to play that game 'I went to the shop and bought ...' We also got to sleep sometimes if it wasn't too noisy, but there was always something going on and it was hard to switch off when there was fun to be had.

We saw quite a few of the same people who came to see us when we were in *The X Factor*. We will always make the effort to go and see our fans if we have time. Sometimes we're being rushed from one place to the next and security won't let us stop, but any time we can, we do.

SUPER STYLIN'

✳ **PERRIE:** I absolutely love clothes and experimenting with them. I love my Doc Martins, my jeans, my pretty tops, my headbands, my jewellery … I couldn't live without any of them.

I would describe my style as kind of rocky and boho. I have a rocky edge with my Doc Martins and my leathers, but I've got a boho style with my hippy dresses and headbands. I love flower power, and I've got three pairs of flowery Doc Martins that I wear all the time. I tend to shop mostly in Topshop, Urban Outfitters, vintage shops, River Island, Schuh and Office. We've all got very different styles so we very rarely share clothes unless it's a vest top or a pair of shorts or something.

We've been given some amazing things since the show. I was given a baggy cream jumper with a big black cross on the front, which I love and wear a lot. I love my OnePiece as well. There's nothing more cosy, and they're so easy to bung on if you're in a rush.

I've got a real passion for shoes, and at the moment I really want to get a pair of New Rocks boots. They're biker boots and they're black with silver buckles on them. They do some massive ones, but I want the ones that are pretty tame, to wear with dresses and things. One item of footwear I would never wear is flip-flops. Even the thought of them makes me feel sick. I don't know why anyone likes them. And socks and sandals? Forget it. Why do people do that? It looks so awful!

I'm quite open about the fact that I've made some bad fashion mistakes in the past. Haven't we all? Quite often when I wake up I don't care what I look like, so I'll

just grab anything and put it on – which results in some interesting outfits. I used to wear some awful stuff when I was younger too, but I blame my mum for that, because some of the things she dressed me in were awful. Mind you, when it was left up to me it wasn't any better. I had no idea how to put things together when I was a kid, so I used to wear stripy tights with a polka-dot t-shirt and things that totally clashed.

I've had a few dodgy haircuts too, my *X Factor* makeover chop being one of them. Once when I was about four I gave myself really short hair and it looked dreadful. It was down to my bum and I chopped the whole lot off. I look back now and wonder why.

My top style icons are Kelly Kapowski, from the TV show *Saved by the Bell*, and Fearne Cotton – I really like her style because she takes chances. I think everyone should wear what they want and not worry about what people say. If you're trying to dress for other people it really shows.

Beauty wise, I love MAC make-up because they have the best colours. I've always admired the model Twiggy, so I look to her and how she used to do her make-up. I think mascara is great, and I love drawing on my bottom eyelashes. Both of those things make your eyes look really big and give your face a focal point.

JESY: I have a massive passion for clothes, and I would say that my style

----

BELOW: Jesy's pre-stage ritual: rubbing her shoes on a towel soaked in Coca-Cola to make sure she doesn't slip on stage

is quite eclectic and mad. I like wearing bright colours and taking risks. I probably shop most in River Island, Topshop and the Adidas shop, but I love discovering new places too. My absolute must-haves are leggings. I literally live in them and wear them with everything. They're so easy and comfy. You won't ever catch me wearing hot pants, though. They look really good on some people, but I'm definitely not a fan.

I'd say that Jessie J and Gwen Stefani are my main style icons, but at the moment the thing I've mostly got my eye on is Perrie's new leather jacket. She got it from eBay and it's vintage and amazing. It's got gold leather studs all over it and it's really old-school and wonderful. I want one just like it, but it's pretty much a one-off. So I may try and borrow it every now and again.

We got given some brilliant clothes when we were on the show, including some great trainers. I also got invited to go along to Fiorelli in London and pick some clothes. I got a lovely jumpsuit and some really nice heels which will be perfect for a night out.

I don't want to have a go at *The X Factor*, because I did like a lot of our outfits, but some of them were things I would never wear and were a bit dubious! I also wasn't a big fan of my *X Factor* hairstyle. It wasn't terrible, but I didn't love it. I was glad to be able to dye it red after the show had finished. Mind you, it's definitely not the worst hairstyle I've ever had. When I was in my early teens I used to wear my hair up in a really tight, slicked-back ponytail and it looked so awful.

Beauty wise, I love Benefit lip glosses and Shu Uemura eyelashes. If you want your eyes to look bigger, definitely wear false eyelashes. They work brilliantly.

I think the most important thing when it comes to style is to wear what you feel comfortable in. Not all fashions are going to suit everyone, so don't follow the crowd – find your own look.

LEIGH-ANNE: I like comfortable stuff generally, but I love getting dressed up if I'm going out. If I'm going to a premiere or something and I'm wearing a dress, I like it to be something unusual, so I stand out. I'd say I'm quite urban and cool.

River Island, Choice, Bank, Topshop and Office are some of my absolute favourite shops. I shop all the time – it's getting a bit out of control! I never borrow clothes from the other girls because I've got so many. I hate wearing things twice, so I end up going out and buying new stuff, but it's got to stop.

We got some amazing freebies when we were on *The X Factor*, which is always lovely. I love my OnePiece, and I also got some great skin stuff from places like Dermalogica and Yonka. I suffer with my skin sometimes, so that's been great. I've also been given 50 per cent off Aqua dresses for life, which is brilliant as I always wear them.

We wore some good stuff on *The X Factor*, but I hated the outfit we had when we performed 'Super Bass'. I know what I like fashion-wise, and I would never wear Doc Martins. I know the other girls like them, but they're not me at all. I hate leather clothes as well, so you won't see me in a biker jacket any time soon. I do want some Jimmy Choo shoes, though. I've never owned any and it would be nice just to say I had a pair!

The Fresh Prince is my main style icon, and I love trainers, high-tops and old-school fashion. I also wear a lot of Rihanna tops – literally tops with Rihanna on them! – and snap back hats. If I were to recommend a look it would be bright jeans, high-tops, snap backs and a Rihanna jumper, because they always look cool. But follow your own rules and wear what you feel good in.

I love bright make-up, so I often wear MAC make-up because they do brilliant colours. But if I had to give one beauty tip, it would be this. Always wash your make-up off before bed, and use a flannel to exfoliate. And *always* moisturise. That's three!

JADE: I think I'm quite geeky and urban when it comes to what I wear. I love bow ties and braces, and I love trainers. I couldn't do without bows or braces now. They're like my 'thing' and I've got so many. Someone even sent me a green flashing bow tie for St Patrick's Day. I really like Labrinth's style, because he wears some really cool gear and also a lot of bow ties, but if I want to wear something I'll just wear it whatever.

I like to be quirky and cool, and have a bit of a cute edge with my glasses – which are real! – and things. I love Urban Outfitters, and I really like Adidas, Nike, Office and Schuh for trainers. At the moment I'm on the lookout for some purple trainers to match my hair!

It's great being in a band with three other girls, because you can borrow their clothes. I'm probably the worst for that – I do it all the time. I even stole Leigh-Anne's shorts and top at Bootcamp to wear for an audition. When we're shopping we often end up buying the same things by mistake, so we have to be careful that we don't all turn up in the same outfit!

We got given a lot of great trainers when we were on the show, and some really cool Little Mix necklaces. I also got given a jumper with my name on which I was very excited about.

I would say that my worst fashion mistake ever was in Week 1 of *The X Factor*. I think it's safe to say that high-waisted, shiny gold leggings do not suit me. I've got the skinniest legs, so when I wore them on stage I looked like a gold toothpick. I would never wear a hippy skirt either. I think it would look totally ridiculous on me.

I haven't always got it right when it comes to beauty either. I had a bob with a fringe when I was a kid, and because my hair is naturally curly it was pinging out all over the place, so I had to straighten it loads. I also used to slick all my hair back and just have two bits of my fringe hanging down. It wasn't good. As for my number one beauty tip? Cocoa butter every time. I use it every day and it makes your skin smell amazing.

FLYING INTO THE FUTURE

JADE: We've got so many great plans for the future. We're really solid as a group now and we totally believe in ourselves. I feel like I've grown up so much over the last year and learnt a million things. It's time for a big new girl band, and hopefully that will be us. We want to be here for a long, long time.

JESY: I want Little Mix to have a number one album and our own tour within two years. I want everyone to love our music. We want to be really accessible. I genuinely see myself doing this job forever, and I want to be successful and happy. I want to wake up every morning knowing I'm doing what I adore.

PERRIE: We want to be as big as the Spice Girls. We're doing what we love and we're so willing to work hard to get to where we want to be. We're living the dream and we don't want it to end any time soon. We want to get the message across that anyone can do what we're doing if they just believe in themselves. We want girls to look up to us, and we want them to feel as good about themselves as they possibly can – and we hope our music can help.

LEIGH-ANNE: I want us to go global. I want us to be the biggest girl band in the world. I want us to take over and create something that's never been done before. I don't just want us to be a good girl band – I want us to be iconic. I look at Lady Gaga and what she's done, and I want us to put our stamp on the music business. We want to be innovators. And we want you to enjoy every minute of the ride with us!

THE BIG LITTLE MIX Q&A

NAME: 🎀 JADE THIRWALL
D.O.B.: 26/12/1992
STAR SIGN: Capricorn

Favourite ...

BOOK: I love reading. I just read *The Girl with the Dragon Tattoo*, which was really good.
FILM: My granddad's favourite was a TV film called *Who Will Love My Children?*, and now my mam and I love it.
BODY PART: My flat tummy.
FOOD: Lasagne and biscuits. But not together.
ALBUM: I really like Beyoncé's *I Am* album.
CELEBRITY BOY: Labrinth. I like his style.
DRINK: Water.
COLOUR: Purple and teal.
T.V. SHOW: *Family Guy* or any quiz show. I'm really good at them.
BREAKFAST: Tea and biscuits.
MEMORY: Winning *The X Factor*. It was an incredible moment.
PERFUME: Sean John, Unforgivable.
PHONE APP: I don't have any, because my phone is really old. I want this app my friend's got where you draw something and the other person has to guess what it is. It's brilliant.
MOTTO FOR LIFE: No day but today.
WAY TO SPEND A SUNDAY: Sunday roast with the family, going to see my dad and my grandparents and then watching films with my mam.
DATE VENUE: I like going for a drive and then going somewhere quirky and funny.
COUNTRY: Australia. I've got family there and it's amazing. It's so relaxed compared to England.
RESTAURANT: My mam's house!
WAY TO RELAX: Being at home with my mam. Having a nice long bath, then watching films and eating loads of rubbish.

NIGHT OUT: Going out in South Shields with my friends. There are a couple of nightclubs and we always go to one called Dusk. It's great because it's small and you always know everyone in there.
WHAT DO YOU NEVER LEAVE THE HOUSE WITHOUT? Gel eyeliner.
WHAT DO YOU KEEP IN YOUR BEDSIDE TABLE? My phone, my make-up bag, a glass of water and photos of my family and friends.
LAST FIVE THINGS YOU BOUGHT: Amy Winehouse's *Lioness* album, an ice-cream, a lasagne, some flowers and some clothes from Urban Outfitters.
WHAT TYPE OF GUY DO YOU LIKE? Guys with swag who dress quite urban. It would be perfect if I could find a boyfriend who wore bow ties, but they're quite rare. I like tattoos and boys who can dance as well. If you can't dance, forget it!

NAME: 📻 JESY NELSON
D.O.B.: 30/09/1991
STAR SIGN: Libra

Favourite ...

BOOK: *A Child Called It* by Dave Pelzer.
FILM: *Taken*. It's so brilliant, everyone should watch it.
BODY PART: My bum. I've got quite a big bum but it's quite peachy.
FOOD: TGI Friday's.
ALBUM: Beyoncé *4*.
CELEBRITY BOY: Plan B or James Corden. James is such a nice guy.
DRINK: Oreo Milkshake.
COLOUR: I like every colour. I love colour.
T.V. SHOW: *Friends*. I never get bored of it and it makes me happy.
BREAKFAST: Poached eggs on toast.
MEMORY: The first time we performed

for the live shows. I was so nervous but so excited. We really had a lot to prove, because we were the bookies' favourites to go and no one expected us to do well, so it was brilliant to show people what we could do.

PERFUME: Juicy Couture.

PHONE APP: BBM.

MOTTO FOR LIFE: Be who you are.

WAY TO SPEND A SUNDAY: I love it when it's cold and rainy outside and I'm cosied up on the sofa watching a film.

DATE VENUE: Going for a walk around London late at night when it's snowing, then going to a nice restaurant.

COUNTRY: So far, Barbados. It's beautiful and the people are so nice.

RESTAURANT: Nando's.

WAY TO RELAX: Chilling with my girls and watching a film.

NIGHT OUT: Going clubbing with friends or going to the cinema.

WHAT DO YOU NEVER LEAVE THE HOUSE WITHOUT?
My hair extensions.

WHAT DO YOU KEEP IN YOUR BEDSIDE TABLE?
My phone.

LAST FIVE THINGS YOU BOUGHT:
A cap, a pair of leggings, a top, some shampoo and some Dr Dre headphones.

WHAT TYPE OF GUY DO YOU LIKE?
I like a guy who's a bit of a geezer, but also funny and romantic.

NAME: LEIGH-ANNE PINNOCK

D.O.B.: 4/10/1991

STAR SIGN: Libra

Favourite ...

BOOK: *A Child Called It* by Dave Pelzer.

FILM: I've got so many, but for a classic film it's *Titanic*.

BODY PART: My bum. I've had a lot of compliments on it because it's very peachy and round.

FOOD: Nachos with everything on them.

ALBUM: Rihanna *Talk That Talk*.

CELEBRITY BOY: Justin Bieber.

DRINK: Malibu and Coke.

COLOUR: Green.

T.V. SHOW: *Waterloo Road*.

BREAKFAST: A bowl of melon with a *pain au chocolat*. I also love toast and lemon curd and a cup of tea.

MEMORY: Singing 'Viva Forever' by the Spice Girls to my nanny. She's not here any more, and it's one of the few times I can remember singing to her. We sang it with Tulisa on *The X Factor*, and Biff, who wrote the song, was in the room. I started crying and everyone thought it was because I didn't like the song, but it was just such a touching moment for me.

PERFUME: Gucci Guilty.

PHONE APP: BBM.

MOTTO FOR LIFE: Just believe.

WAY TO SPEND A SUNDAY: Having a Sunday roast cooked by my mum and then watching the *EastEnders* repeat.

DATE VENUE: A walk on the beach under the stars, because I love stars.

COUNTRY: Jamaica or Barbados.

RESTAURANT: Vodka Revolutions. They do the best nachos.

WAY TO RELAX: Listening to or playing slow jams. And having a nice massage.

NIGHT OUT: At Anaya in London.

WHAT DO YOU NEVER LEAVE THE HOUSE WITHOUT? My iPod and my Beats.

WHAT DO YOU KEEP IN YOUR BEDSIDE TABLE?
My phone, for my alarm.

LAST FIVE THINGS YOU BOUGHT:
A dress to go out in, two pencil skirts, a new Rihanna jumper, a headband and a onesie from Republic.

WHAT TYPE OF GUY DO YOU LIKE?
Clean-shaven, cute looking, toned, muscly, funny and sensitive.

NAME: ✳ **PERRIE EDWARDS**
D.O.B.: 10/07/1993
STAR SIGN: Cancer

Favourite ...

BOOK: I think the first book I ever read will be Little Mix's!

FILM: I'm a proper movie geek and I love all films, but I'll say *The Notebook*.

BODY PART: My eyes, because blue is my favourite colour.

FOOD: Anything. I love all food, although I'm not too keen on cheese.

ALBUM: Ed Sheeran's +, and Journey's *Greatest Hits*.

CELEBRITY BOY: Johnny Depp. He's the man.

DRINK: Apple juice.

COLOUR: Blue.

T.V. SHOW: *The OC* or *Friends*. *Friends* is hilarious and I watched it all the time when I was growing up. My all-time favourite show is *Saved by the Bell*. I'm obsessed with it and I've got all the box sets.

BREAKFAST: Full English, or waffles with bacon and syrup and ice-cream.

MEMORY: I've got so many, but with the band it was the week we all spent together at my house in Newcastle.

PERFUME: Christine Aguilera. I don't know what it smells like, because I have no sense of smell, but whenever I wear it everyone says it's gorgeous.

PHONE APP: My guitar tuner.

MOTTO FOR LIFE: Good things come to those who wait, but faster yet to those who take. And also, don't worry, be hippy!

WAY TO SPEND A SUNDAY:
Having my nanna's Sunday dinner, a good movie and a nap in front of the fire.

DATE VENUE: The beach, either when it's nice and sunny and we're in shorts and sunhats, or when it's cold and the stars are out and we're all wrapped up.

COUNTRY: Hong Kong. It's amazing.

RESTAURANT: Any all-you-can-eat buffets.

WAY TO RELAX: On holiday, beside the pool with my headphones on.

NIGHT OUT: A girlie night out getting food.

WHAT DO YOU NEVER LEAVE THE HOUSE WITHOUT?
My phone.

WHAT DO YOU KEEP IN YOUR BEDSIDE TABLE?
A glass of water. I'm always thirsty.

LAST FIVE THINGS YOU BOUGHT: A pair of red Doc Martins, my vintage leather jacket, a playsuit, a headband and some jewellery.

WHAT TYPE OF GUY DO YOU LIKE?
Nice and tanned and rugged. No one too pretty. I like a guy who takes pride in his appearance but isn't too clean cut.

Here's the juicy stuff!
Out of all of us who is the ...

Messiest?

JADE: We are all very messy. Our room in the *X Factor* house was absolutely trashed.

JESY: We're all as messy as each other.

LEIGH-ANNE: No, it's me, definitely. I've been trying to be better, though.

PERRIE: We are all pretty messy. Jesy needs the most room for all of her stuff, but she is quite organised. She had seven cases when we started on the *X Factor* tour.

Funniest?

LEIGH-ANNE: We're all really funny, but Jesy is the funniest.

PERRIE: I agree – Jesy.

JADE: Jesy is really funny when she's in a good mood. She's really good at doing characters and accents.

JESY: I'd say Leigh-Anne.

Moodiest?

JESY: Me. I'm either really happy or really moody. There's no in between with me.

LEIGH-ANNE: Jesy. If she's in a mood, stay away.

PERRIE: Yes, that's Jesy again.

JADE: She is either the happiest, funniest person in the world, or the snappiest. You can totally tell when she's switching, so you know to run away or be quiet.

Sexiest?

JESY: I reckon Leigh-Anne.

PERRIE: I'll say Leigh-Anne too.

LEIGH-ANNE: I probably wear the most revealing stuff, but I reckon it's Jesy because she's got great boobs.

JADE: I'll say Jesy too. She's got amazing boobs and an amazing bum.

The peacemaker?

JESY: Leigh-Anne.

JADE: If we ever have a little bicker Leigh-Anne makes sure we sort it out and move on.

LEIGH-ANNE: Me or Perrie. I've never bickered with Perrie. If any of us bicker it's forgotten in five minutes.

PERRIE: I am pretty good at being a peacemaker, but I don't have to do it very often.

The sensitive one?

LEIGH-ANNE: Jesy.

PERRIE: Jesy.

JADE: Jesy.

JESY: Yes, probably me and sometimes Perrie.

Most annoying?

JESY: Perrie when she burps.

LEIGH-ANNE: Jesy when she gets up early to do her hair while I'm trying to sleep.

PERRIE: That drives me mad too. I love to sleep and there's no way I can if Jesy is up and about.

JADE: Perrie annoys me at times by putting herself down for her singing – when it's incredible.

When was the last time you argued?

LEIGH-ANNE: When I tried to get Jesy to turn the hairdryer off!

JESY: But we don't really argue about it. I just carry on.

PERRIE: I've never had an argument with any of the girls. We've bickered but there's never been a proper argument.

JADE: I told Perrie off for thinking she'd performed a rubbish show when she hadn't, but it certainly was not an argument.

Whose time-keeping is worst?

LEIGH-ANNE: Mine or Jesy's.

JESY: I'd say Perrie or Jade.

PERRIE: I'm going to say Jesy. I get up late but I'm still somehow always on time.

JADE: Jesy missed the tour bus a couple of times because she was late. It drove off without her, so I think that says it all.

Who's the best at chatting up guys?

LEIGH-ANNE: Jesy's a big flirt.

PERRIE: Jesy is an amazing flirt. She does it in a nice, cute way.

JESY: No, Leigh-Anne is a bigger flirt than me!

JADE: Leigh-Anne is quite good at chatting up. She's got very seductive eyes.

Who is best at problem solving?

LEIGH-ANNE: Me and Jade.

JESY: Jade. She's so clever.

PERRIE: Jade is really good, but so is Jesy. She says it like it is.

JADE: I think we can all be good at that. If any of us has got a problem we'll help each other until it's all sorted out.

Who's most likely to fall asleep in the middle of work?

LEIGH-ANNE: Jesy.

JESY: Perrie. Actually, I have done it as well, but Perrie sleeps even more than me.

PERRIE: I think Jesy is worse than me!

JADE: Jesy fell asleep in a meeting with our accountant once!

Can you tell us any secrets about the others?

LEIGH-ANNE: Jesy turns from Jekyll into Hyde when she's in a mood, Jade loves doing Sudoku, and Perrie farts when she's nervous.

JESY: Leigh-Anne fancies Bieber.

JADE: Jesy is always first in the make-up chair at shows. She'll literally elbow us out of the way!

PERRIE: Leigh-Anne is a total practical joker.

BELOW: Getting excited before going on stage

THANK YOU

We would like to thank all of the team at *The X Factor*, Sid and Beth and all the producers on the show.

A big thank you to all the crew that made it happen, and in particular all the researchers who looked after us and made the experience so much more fun and less stressful. Thank you to all of the judges for the constructive comments you gave us, which helped us strive to improve each week.

Simon, Sonny, Emma, Guy, Anya, Mark and everyone at Syco and Sony - thank you for all your help it's very much appreciated.

Thank you to everyone who helped us create the best album possible for our fans. The writers, the producers...

Simon Jones we would have never been able to deal with press without you. Alan, Barry and Elaine at Live Wire Business Management, thank you for all your hard work. A big thank you also to Josh Smith, our fantastic lawyer.

Sophie, Adam, Nicki and Zoe - thank you for helping us magically scrub up so well even on those dreaded early mornings!

A huge thank you to Dean Freeman for your dedication to this project and your beautiful photos! Thank you also to Richard Poulton and Joby Ellis. Thank you to Natalie Jerome, Victoria McGeown and the whole team at HarperCollins. We are so happy to have made our first book with you. Thank you for all the time and energy you have put into making our first book just the way we had always dreamed!

Modest Management - our managers Richard and Harry, Katie, Sheema, Jane,

Natalie and everyone else at Modest! Thank you for all the hard work and effort you put into us - it never goes unnoticed.

We owe Annecka, our manager, hundreds of thank yous. You are the fifth Little Mixer. You never stop guiding us and you've been the best mentor we could ask for. Thank you Grace for being a friend as well as our assistant manager and making us laugh non-stop.

Last but not least, Tulisa, thank you for believing in us throughout the competition and making our dreams come true. You will always play a big part in our lives, WE LOVE YOU!!

LEIGH-ANNE: Wow, what an incredible journey this has been for me. Within the space of a year everything I have ever dreamed of has come true.

Mum and Dad, my heroes; your support and belief are what got me through those times when I didn't think the dream was possible. I love you both so much, I hope I've made you proud. My sisters and inspirations, Sarah and Sian; growing up it was you guys who I aspired to be like. Thank you for everything you have done for me and for believing in me when others didn't. We showed them, eh?!

To all my amazing friends and family, you have shown me such an unbelievable amount of support not just throughout *X Factor* but through every single talent show and performance I ever took part in leading up to this moment.

I have met some of the most amazing people this year including my three new sisters: Jesy, Perrie and Jade. I want to thank these girls as they have brought the best out of me. Thank you for making this

the most incredible year of my life. I LOVE YOU FOREVER.

To our incredible fans, without you none of this would have been possible. To every single Little Mixer who picked up the phone and voted for us, from the bottom of my heart, thank you!

Just believe

JADE: This has been the best year ever and for this I have so many people to thank, right from my childhood until now. If I forget anyone please don't be offended!

My first thank you is for my mam who is my best friend, my rock, my inspiration and the strongest, most selfless person I know. Thank you for doing everything you possibly could to help me achieve my dream.

My dad for always being there for me and being the best taxi driver in the world! My brother Karl who has always believed in me and every day makes me so proud. My auntie Norma and my nanna and granddad for all their support. My granddad Mohammed who isn't here anymore but always gave me the confidence to be who I wanted to be.

Holly and Anna, my best friends, who have been there for me through thick and thin. And all of my family and friends for their continuing support.

Everyone who gave me the opportunity to perform and gig before this journey, without you I wouldn't be in this position now.

My teachers who taught me that if you work hard and are determined you can do anything.

Thank you to the North East, particularly south Tyneside, for supporting myself and Perrie before, during and hopefully after *The X Factor*! Your support means so much and I know a lot of our success is down to you.

Perrie, Leigh and Jesy for changing my life and giving me the confidence I didn't have on my own. I wouldn't want to experience this with anybody else and I can't wait to share my future with them.

Thank you to all of the fans – we owe so much to you. Thank you to the fans who believed in us from the beginning, the fans who joined us along the way and the fans we continue to gain. Each and every one of you is so important to us because, quite frankly, you're the reason we've come so far. Thank you for picking us up whenever we've felt down, and for sticking up for us no matter what! Thanks for being friends as well as fans; whenever I miss home, or just feel like laughing, I look at your comments and support and everything feels fine again. We are so grateful and proud to have such dedicated fans – we love you Little Mixers!

And lastly, thank you to the inventors of the bow, the brace and the biscuit. I salute you.

JESY: The first person I would like to say thank you to is my mumma, because if it wasn't for her believing in me and encouraging me to follow my dreams I would never be where I am now. She is the most incredible woman I know and I can't thank her enough for everything that she does for me; so thank you Mumma for being amazing and being in my life. I love you so so much.

The next person I would like to thank is my sister Jade, for also believing in me and encouraging me to audition for *The X Factor*. She is my best friend, as cheesy as that sounds, and I love her very much.

I also want to thank my two brothers, my nan and granddad, auntie Jo and cousin Jamie for supporting me throughout this whole experience. You have been amazing and I love you all lots.

I want to thank all of my friends for being there with me through this journey. My Soli bubs Dilem, Esin and Elouise, you're the most amazing friends – you believed and encouraged me to follow my dreams. I can't thank you enough.

My next thank you is to my three beautiful best friends who have actually made my life; Lee Lee, Jade and Pezza. I couldn't live without you girls, you are my family now and have made this whole experience so incredible. I don't know what I would do without you so THANK YOU for helping to make my dream come true. I am so proud of us.

Last but not least I would like to thank our amazing fans - without you guys we wouldn't be where we are now, you have changed our lives and we can't thank you enough for your incredible support. We love you so so much and hope we continue to make music that you love and enjoy.

PERRIE: Writing these thank yous is the hardest part of the book! I have that many incredible people in my life that I don't even know where to start.

My mam is obviously my world! She has always been my inspiration, even when I was small. From her singing, to her personality, to her strength, I've never met a woman so strong and wise. She's incredible and has always stood by me through everything, whether it was my mistakes or greatest achievements. She's been there through it all and I can't thank her enough!

My dad is like a jester, he's forever making me laugh and hyping me up about my voice, always telling me I can become anything if I put my mind to it. I have such amazingly talented parents, I love em!

A big thank you also to everyone at the RVI hospital in Newcastle, especially Mrs Lawson for making me fit and ready to take on the world in Little Mix! I have my health thanks to this hospital so I can't thank them enough.

I wanna thank my brother Jonnie for being so amazing and always being there for me. I love him for performing with me and playing guitar with me. He really helped us girls before Judges' Houses. He rehearsed and played guitar for us the whole time we stayed in Newcastle. He's the best big brother in the world!

Thank you to my beautiful little sister Caitlin for being such a little gem, supporting me all the way through everything. She always puts a big grin on my face and cheers me up when I'm down.

A big thanks to all my friends and my stepparents Mark and Joanne for their amazing support. My amazing nanas, my aunties, uncles and cousins. We're such a close family and I love them all very much! I am a very lucky girl to have such amazing people around me to keep me grounded and always put a smile on my face. I couldn't ask for a more supportive family. I'm so blessed and I love you all!

A massive thank you to my fruit loop sisters, Lee Lee, Jesy, and Jade – you girls are amazing! You've all helped me so much on this big journey in different ways. I have a lot to thank you for! You always make me laugh and I love you all lots!!

Most importantly I have to say thank you to the fans for getting us where we are. It sounds clichéd but you made our dreams come true. I can't thank you enough for the amazing support; you make us stronger and more dedicated because we wanna do it for you guys. I love you all lots for giving me the opportunity to do what I love for a living.

Peace out!

Dean Freeman is an internationally acclaimed photographer and director, who has published 11 books. Bestsellers such as *Beckham* and *Michael Bublé* have highlighted Dean's unique ability to create timeless and iconic imagery of musicians, singers, sporting icons and artists – his subjects include Katy Perry, George Michael, David Beckham and Leona Lewis. Dean has also worked with major global brands on advertising campaigns.

Freeman captures a sense of urgency and immediacy, creating a need to look and see his images. His photography has a sense of humour and an appreciation for the absurd, but where Freeman truly excels is in detecting the beauty that extends beyond time and place.
–*Nylon* magazine

HarperCollins*Publishers*
77–85 Fulham Palace Road,
Hammersmith, London W6 8JB

www.harpercollins.co.uk

First published by HarperCollins*Publishers* 2012
10 9 8 7 6 5 4 3 2 1

Photography and creative direction by Dean Freeman
Design by Joby Ellis

ISBN   978-0-00-748817-9

Printed and bound in China